Time Being II

Also by Joseph Torra

Fiction

Gas Station
Tony Luongo
My Ground
The Bystander's Scrapbook
They Say
What's So Funny
What It Takes

Poetry

16 Paintings
Domino Sessions
Keep Watching the Sky
August Letter to My Wife and Daughters
After the Chinese
Watteau Sky (with Ed Barrett)
Time Being

Memoir

Call Me Waiter
Who Do You Think You Are?

Time Being II

Joseph Torra

Quale Press

Copyright © 2025 by Joseph Torra

Cover: "The Activity of Nature Never Ceases," a painting by Joseph Torra

The author thanks the editor of *Spoke,* where sections of *Time Being II* previously appeared.

ISBN: 978-1-935835-39-4 trade paperback edition

LCCN: 2025948158

Quale Press
www.quale.com

Time Being II

An improvisation
October 21, 2020 – October 21, 2021

This book is dedicated to all the colleagues and students I worked with in my 20 years of teaching at UMass/Boston

It's said the Tao is formless with no structure yet resonates through everything without form its functions are intuited by observing all things they're ripping up Berkeley Street with jackhammers yellow vested men in hard hats and ear protection Jim text photo a striper caught at Rafe's Chasm for months he's there each morning 5 A.M. fishing swimming watching the sun rise writing his poems reading student short stories haunted cars ghosts narcissistic mothers abusive lovers suicide by oversize toasters fantasy lands princesses castles moats hairy hands x-ray eyes starless skies passive wives futuristic detectives tortured women homeless fathers gamblers horses dog handlers shapechangers last of fall foliage clings to trees how to celebrate Thanksgiving during the pandemic what do alchemical practices elongate if you can breathe something and die child's blue ball stuck in the grapevine that wraps around the fence three cups green tea yoga then banana whole grain toast let the workmen shout my silence drowns them out no I didn't watch the presidential debate it's impossible to explain the vastness of the ocean to a fish living in a tiny puddle Jim writes that Gerrit is the glue binds us all together Amanda writes as a child she walked quietly through the woods as she could Eva writes muddy water becomes clear when undisturbed for a long time I write leaves leave shadows on window panes content without names some hide behind black screens names in white letters never speak a word others display their photos with names others show their faces interact like a real class audios and visuals malfunction technology bounces them out of the meeting never sure if I can get them back in with their personal technological school and work problems what can I do and what should I leave alone Gerrit has a new pool why do you need one Atlantic's across the street he smirks and says hurtful things about my writing mornings steeping tea yoga read papers organize assignments files that won't open in Blackboard emails Zoom meetings texts from friends trapped all of us trapped behind masks that steam my glasses how many more cases how many more deaths I tell her maybe *On the Road* is difficult for Chinese readers without context like American readers trying to read ancient Chinese poetry America 1950s significance of the automobile ability to drive across the country in three days she says thousands of years Pan Ku Lao has hopped on his white donkey to fly across China in seconds bombarded with too many thoughts we're deluded how to quiet the mind aware of my foolishness no small business the baby next door tries to speak words that won't come out right tonight sauce fresh tomatoes basil from the garden over rigatoni don't overeat stop before full don't eat and work at the same time dark load in washer spin cycle unload dishwasher days run seamlessly into each other everything in the universe is connected protected is subjective if it comes who'll get the vaccine and when three houses within the block stripped down to stud daily hammers machines demolition trucks workmen old two-families expanded into three condos real estate great boon of our time the city unrecognizable over decades slick coffee shops eateries young hipsters upscale families too many cars not enough parking higher taxes living costs through the roof hard to maintain a low profile drinking in darkness spewing out light no internet at home she attends five remote classes sitting in her car Dunkin' Donuts parking lot piggy-backing wi-fi writing a novel about her journey from Vietnam to America I want to be a great writer professor she says you don't have to tell the trees to grow or animals to reproduce all part of the natural order of things Amanda sings plays the ukulele every Monday night live from her living room via Zoom pandemic surge promised soon Peter phones test results growths on neck tongue lung difference one month makes the drought continues worst mushroom hunting in memory but walk the woods anyway leaves down smell decay along the trail follow seasons following seasons can't force them in Nature there're no fixed judgements rocks accumulate make a mountain nothing humane about it this activity does not cease oh knowledge never sufficient drop me off at the next stop it is said art begins by evoking fear of the unknown the great clod burdens it with form emerging returning learning not to strive for what life can do nothing about preserve what you already have without stepping outside the door for more the beginning of one thing is usually the ending of another Hugh sends latest files new guitar tracks who knew we could record during the lockdown each in separate quarters playing together as one Julia and Celeste home for Molly's birthday pasta roasted red pepper sauce baked zucchini steak with green peppers and onions chocolate cake mocha butter cream frosting a flower doesn't lose its smell if no one is there to smell it stay well the words of the day writing when invented was used to manage affairs then by fools so not to forget things and the wise to record events later to make falsehoods that free the guilty kill the innocent beyond where there is no beyond is greatest latest polls show Biden ahead of Trump forty percent think there could be civil war talk of the World Series and football heat's finally on still no first frost last tomatoes fruiting on yellowing plants suddenly four inches heavy snow first white Halloween in memory branches and boughs weighed down twenty-five degrees this morning things are never permanent as we think what's reasonable today ludicrous tomorrow no one will remember what I did after I die if I am remembered it will be what others choose to remember my poetry students write their own "I Remember" poems in the manner of Joe Brainard Christmases past lovers mothers ice cream cones brothers cars with flats long lost hats baseball bats ice skating broken lamp first dance first kiss first time she set eyes on him first time he felt her losing one's breath a bruised neck broken toe sprained wrist birthday wishes waves that knock you over growing older setting suns heavy rains sledding in snow letting go reigns dogs cats barn with bats grandparent deaths bicycle wreck broken hearts baked bean farts nearly drowning lost then found spiders abound tripping on ground slipping off a roof smashed window blame happiness sorrow borrowed necklace pain loss loneliness lost in a department store first dates canceled dates last dates sour taste on her lips guilty feelings rich or poor famous or unknown everyone's a pile of bones after death sun and rain all the snow gone days grow a giant hand drags me out of my car parked in an underground garage a voice shouting you should have known this would happen as I'm pulled across the ground reading Amanda Mitch and Jim's brilliant poems accept what you can't get and find there's nourishment in acceptance today's election day long woods walk clear the mind why do stupid people occupy high places in government some very average people rise to great fame and fortune if the timing is right rigid branches break easily so bend in wind and under the weight of ice next spring semester more remote courses the pandemic begins to surge again it is written the universe is not humane temperature hits 70 today two days since the election still no clear winner flap your wings like birds that fly to places with no boundaries step into the Way to why are you going there towards destiny towards death what's short what's long measure to the end of the string yet there is no measure to things the Way has no beginning no end what to do what not to do let it all go knowing sun sets moon rises they follow each other another holiday season you don't have to eat turkey if you don't want or listen to Christmas music or get drunk on New Year's Eve dwelling places of schemes where people search for joy far away from the noisy city sounds never cease wind strums branches waves splash the shoreline ducks quack stir up water taking flight across the lake squirrels rustle dry fallen leaves distant woodpecker working a tree air I breathe sweet pine dying vegetation our nation divided still no word who will be next president yesterday 100,000 new pandemic cases Boston back on curfew stricter restrictions the *Wen-Tzu* teaches that intellectualism eventually runs out of tricks don't spend your life worrying and grieving over the chaos of the world it's like crying into a river to increase its water in fear of it drying up another summer-like day warm temps sunny sky sipping tea reading student poems what advice but keep reading keep writing let your mind go the word will follow it is said memory is the root of human problems forget the past face the future unchain that dog barks in the yard nothing left to guard don't forget your home but roam worldly matters end but you can't stop the tide Jim texts from Rafe's Chasm with John and Gabe blazing sunrise three wise guys the Atlantic crashing on granite slabs everything born of one energy that can't be named fame is fleeting it takes too much to gain hey mister play another song about the man who dwelt in a cave without a name avoiding games died and became immortal they're dancing across America Trump voted out car horns shouts in the streets on the front porch I bang a victory beat on my snare drum first woman vice president ever got a long way to go though good to know some bad things come to an end then it's back to the long feud broke my front tooth on a bone my dentist been warning me for years that row of teeth weak trouble down the road beware of dentists who see the future baby next door cries now speaks full words Mom Mom Mom Dad Dad Dad master the child within yourself but know no master sometimes I think the greatest skills have an appearance of clumsiness every day more invitations to online poetry readings impossible to keep up even if I want to attend which I don't when the pandemic first struck there were no poetry readings now more than ever poets from all over the world on one screen reading to record audiences from all over the world what happened to only four people showing up at reading two of them the readers I fight with a tall bulky man broom sticks our weapons each time I try to make contact he steps aside sticks me in the side and taunts the woman driver didn't see the young man on the scooter he stops in front of her shouts she is a fucking bitch I'm watching closely he notices gives her the finger and

scoots away everyone's so spring-loaded and angry
dentist says I need a bridge row of teeth too old and
brittle gray morning lots of frail brown leaves stick
to branches student flash fiction stories dropping in
it is written that a mass of energy circulates through
the body why cling to local forms or conventions I
watched a sonnet fall into emptiness only to return
confused and degenerate conventional views lead
down misleading paths load of whites in the washer
dishes on rinse cycle I barely keep up with necessary
chores how clean a clean floor why would anybody
want to eat off one below the clouds birds of a feather fly together and beyond that particles of dust
space and time climb the void the Way their guide
if you close up inside there's nowhere to enter yoga
is unity the mind a microcosm of the universe the
universe a macrocosm of the mind the Great Clod
burdens me with form belabors me with life eases
me with age releases me in death I only borrow this
breath neighborhood walk shadows emerge and
return in car headlights people arrive home from
work open windows this warm evening smell garlic
curry peppers onions meat fish bits of conversation
jazz rock hip-hop folk Spanish music all float in the
air Christmas lights early this year houses apartments balconies lit up leaves blow around my feet
up along these busy streets exposed bedrock and
backyard ledges date back 600,000 years up and

over Central Hill work up a low sweat down Highland Ave. back to Central Street past the neighbors to home honey mustard chicken cheesy rice steamed broccoli Julia swings by drops off scented candles drive her home through Davis Square abuzz with people restaurants and bars filled to social distance capacities everybody in close quarters eat drink mask-less the pandemic continues to spread people desperate to socialize this morning rusty water through pipes email the Water Department no word back act with cool clarity rather than impulse it has been said that Westerners lack the cultural basis for practicing Eastern disciplines perhaps there is truth in this important thing's to ignore blind imitation water runs clearly again I'm riding a bicycle through a hilly suburban neighborhood well-landscaped yards sculpted shrubs vast flower beds birdbaths long lawns yard to yard the bike rolls up and over any obstacle dogs everywhere chase after me growl trying to bite I remain out of reach eventually arrive at an ocean beach bog down in sand hounds surround me move in for the kill accept shortcomings don't bear grudges good words and actions can sometimes be empty show lost count the last time I counted found numbers not enough to add up to each word always in perpetual flight always on to something else a generative process through which things arise and pass away some leaves cling to trees right through winter Celeste and Julia joint email with Thanksgiving menu Molly will bake pies cancel classes the day before the holiday give students and myself a break I miss the interaction of the classroom writing on the board students hiding in the back busy on their cell phones long lines at the food kiosks waiting for bad food students and colleagues hello in the hallways and rushing across campus from one class to another vaccine on the way not soon enough over a quarter of a million dead across the country some still insist the pandemic a hoax refuse masks boast about rights and freedom visiting New York staying at Mitch Highfill's a big studio unusable steam punk machinery strewn everywhere Mitch off to work I'm waiting for him Joey and Dee Dee Ramone arrive they are friends with Mitch Dee Dee strums a guitar Joey sings new songs they just wrote together then Dee Dee wants to go to his apartment to do drugs but Joey doesn't then Bill Corbett is giving me Pressed Wafer books and Ed Barrett is there but I already have all the books he offers me Bill's over seven feet tall thin with big bandage over a stomach wound he says same height he's always been I give him a gentle hug goodbye this morning pot of green tea read papers on Ralph Ellison's "Battle Royal" and poems about place a short story from an MA student's creative writing thesis then break for my own writing before yoga

Trump hasn't conceded the election sun breaks through clouds above neighbors' slanted rooftops drone of lonely jet Julia comes for supper baked salmon pasta pesto sauteed broccoli pistachio ice cream talk of Trump Churchill Stalin Mao colonization new Netflix series *Black Friday* Christmas shopping plan Thanksgiving menu no turkey again this year fine with me fine with me fine with me everyone chimes in Hinton writes that each word needs to operate at the very origin-moment word and thing emerging into existence simultaneously 24 degrees this morning it's said this will be a mild winter bald eagles spotted along the Mystic River in Somerville wild turkey overrun our streets stop traffic perch atop fences next thing you know bears will be trouncing trash cans when humans disappear how long before Somerville is wild again and buildings collapse the Mystic River run clear a few centuries ago the Massachusetts tribe roamed here hunted fished until Chief Nanepashemet killed by settlers in a raid his window deeded this land for 21 coats 19 fathoms of wampum and 3 bushels of corn kind of puts a damper on Thanksgiving early morning market run for Molly's baking flower sugar vanilla extract apples butter heavy cream eggs pumpkin market's quiet readying for the big rush later today the Way provides an emotional framework to move through the world writing enacts an awakening in the end words are not simply about apparent content heater dries the air in the house put humidifier inside acoustic guitar prevent wood from cracking if horses are meant to run free why put them in a comfortable stable able to see the Tao in many different ways know you cannot see the Tao consciousness is woven wholly into the Cosmos forget those colors that once painted the mind behind each brushstroke blossoms clot the story of our lives emptying into sky the ancients wrote the world is what we make of it we create happiness and sorrows burrow into the ground learn to ride the wind therein an act of one thing causes effects in another we don't know where feelings come from or where they go you know Molly's apple pie for breakfast wild turkey in front of Dunkin' Donuts won't move parking lot jammed car horns blare people take cell phone photos young woman with red beret and miniature dog barking man with long ladder over his shoulder trotting down the sidewalk stops we do this we do that Randy guest my short story class reads his story about humility Mitch guest in poetry class says survival isn't happiness open the heart forget the clock walk over clouds into sky Grace Slick sang the human race doesn't mean shit to a tree absence and presence are simply different ways of seeing float drift attack strike all words can function as any kind of speech I reach into my heart grab what's hauled in from a wide-cast net more jets flying than usual holiday travel against warnings experts predict thousands more dead for tradition turkey booze and pie inside my mind I see stars from eons ago blazing here and now rainy gray Thanksgiving morning apple pie for breakfast Julia and Celeste awake early prepare dinner homemade fettuccine carbonara fresh baked rolls salad French onion soup apple pie chocolate pumpkin torte Beverly Corbett email sends love and holiday wishes how many Thanksgivings past at 9 Columbus Square much wine food cheer so many old and new friends years pass nothing lasts except memory when the moon arrives I open the door allow her in the weave of dark and light empty mind empty sight blood turns to water human affairs inhabit absence emerge into presence words develop little individual identities that blur together into shared conscious space like the awakened Cosmos contained in a tiny raindrop softly now hear pitter patter matter sung in a song returned to brilliance that never ceases house to house gossip under roofbeams who says what who went where who told when how to catch me if you can in the business of quiet mystery internet service down from holiday overload listen to music recordings stored on my desktop music files old Box Willie Alexander Fireking The First Supper put trapped dead mouse in trash night sky's star-grained expanse shines down into my body fluids floods over subsuming things into the single whole where form and formlessness muddle indifferent to our human concerns assumptions about the nature of things around us and our relationship to them what falls what startles up in the existential night at some point there's simply nothing more to say tomato sauce simmers on stove with meatballs mushrooms ziti with lines still more apple pie left news of Bob's death friend of 30 years found in his shower been there for days things are never permanent as we wish lose the sky loosen the world clouds ground into powder and eaten help build strong men wearing women's old clothes wandering drunk carrying flowers only to disappear where are you then sipping tea early morning sun-burst through windows continued warm temps putting one word in front of another who reads cloud script traverses the 9 city blocks you don't need an immortal riding a white donkey down Somerville Ave. but it helps roofs slant chimneys lean layers of shingles travel in circles I cannot force the direction of things music's a bridge that helps us communicate with our hearts and minds hear with your eyes see with your ears it's good to know how to withdraw when the work's finished the phenomena of the world are fleeting the moment you point to them they are gone once upon a time I believed I could hold them until they made something new and wonderful drop that thought look inside yourself catch the law of nature with a radiant blade cutting through illusions things merely occur until we give them meaning do you really need others to consider virtuous to be virtuous I fell off the ladder everyone felt better heavy rain and wind knocked over Molly's garden supplies on the front porch pots filled with soil tools and shelving unit water in the basement no mice since I bought new traps internet's out three times in four days Sunnylyn's new book in the mail the energy in our bodies is the energy of the universe get caught up in too many choices you'll be confused don't worry about status nothing is superior or inferior it is said the Way can be achieved when consciousness ceases final push of the semester stories poems essays drop students tired depressed anxious desperate behind their Zoom screens stuck inside their dwellings cramming for exams staying up all night to write papers missing their families and friends the sky is a blue dome in which I roam gathering debris that floats freely for the taking deep in the earth inhabitants that visit us in dreams seems one day is an eon depending on how you look at it all events send ripples through creation the activity of Nature never ceases life and death an illusion hair today bald tomorrow Jupiter and Saturn close in on each other two more weeks they'll appear as one patterns recur observed pick Julia up go to buy our Christmas trees three foot one for her apartment seven foot for the house Molly saw another mouse even though we have trapped four must be a nest the nurse practitioner says I have some kind of bacterial infection on my skin itchy for days script for an antibiotic stop scratching rub calamine lotion to prevent the itch whether you're rich or not depends on how you think about it the Way cannot be discovered by conscious thinking I wish I could empty my mind throw away my knowledge but I am only able to talk about it final classes meet today ten days to read papers and projects post grades email lighting up students requesting extensions myriad reasons and excuses give them until the end of the week first time in UMass Boston history the entire school gone remote learning you've made history I tell them and one more semester to go as long as the pandemic vaccine comes through as promised over a quarter of a million Americans have died since March and people still demand their right not to lockdown or wear masks in the name of freedom I'm dancing with Margo the band loud she laughs shouting over the music jumps up on stage dances with the band the crowd cheers big smile wide so happy with herself she leaps onto a group of people they drop her but she bounces up unhurt the Tao has no direction no front or back no left or right it lies within the universe but no one knows where notice without looking hear without listening Julia comes for dinner decorate the tree baked ziti and ice cream Celeste wins first place for her class project I can't stop thinking of my children they killed one of the wild turkeys because it kept attacking people three-hour dentist appointment assess how much work must be done to my bottom teeth extractions crowns and bridges to the tune of twelve thousand dollars in a tiny rowboat fishing on Wrights Pond surface mirror-still so clear I can see the bottom drop my worm down drift slowly where the current takes me to the other side brand new concrete complexes when did they build those a voice from shore shouts all the fish are gone you're wasting your time suddenly I'm paddling with my feet and the boat begins to float in the air hovers over the water antibiotic has cleared my bacterial skin infection no more itching the rashes fading Lao-tzu said to have knowledge and do nothing has the same merit as having no knowledge await word from eastern sky until the drizzle charcoal lines the way shadow falls wind really something today that creaky old pine so many deities biggest snow storm in years shovel four hours dig out both cars pull arm muscle lower back aches anarchist conference communal house in California stream runs underneath exposed through openings in floors everyone friends except for me I have a crush on a woman then she and a man with a long beard are readying for sex in front of us all no one seems to notice except me I get lost on a train on my way to the airport in a public bathroom there's a card game and drug deals you're on the wrong side of town a man tells me the formless practice of turning the light around is repeated daily as the mind becomes fluid and buoyant we practice ordinary activities and don't get stuck on things no matter how hard art tries to imitate Nature Nature does a better job 5 A.M. awake pot of tea plug in Christmas tree Celeste home from school today with biomedical engineering degree don't let a person's words make or break you always something to do and none more worthwhile than another forgetting yourself is not so easy as it sounds especially when bound to tradition so deeply rooted hard to escape its limitations who let this mass of jello loose on the world swirls in unseen spaces without a name light erases false habits shines where you can begin anew Jupiter and Saturn dance together in the Cosmos Christmas Eve day straighten downstairs vacuum put wrapped presents under the tree prepare food for tonight Celeste and Julia home cheeses hard Italian salami sausages and peppers chicken wings fresh vegetables dips crackers good bread fruit wine for Molly hard cider Celeste ginger beer Julia sparkling cider me Molly's baked holiday treats holiday wish texts to and from friends outside kids play in their yard excitedly eager for the day to come to a close and Santa take to the sky guided by Rudolph's red nose childhood staring towards stars out my grandparents North End living room window how possible one man do so much within one night's span can it be true and what about God maybe they lie about him too Christmas morning sheets of rainwater in the basement all snow washed away home-fried potatoes Canadian bacon eggs and Celeste's home-baked buns tea coffee juice open gifts the Tao's where all things gather where everything emanates from it always watches water tea and the quiet post-Christmas day letdown everyone asleep neighborhood tranquil internet down refrigerator creak distant car passing on street four-week break until spring semester too many people in the world think they alone are right eager to pit their wit and cleverness against others but the Way cannot be transmitted by concepts and theory time permanence or illusions so why wait until the guitar store opens at ten to bring my acoustic in for a tune-up why impose seconds minutes hours days weeks months years decades and centuries on nothing the Cosmos doesn't know it is Saturday morning I'm still mourning my mother dead four years this past week she lived to nearly ninety it is said that which gives way to life does not die my mother called oatmeal oak-meal Saturday mornings cooked breakfast sausages and eggs while I watched Magilla the Gorilla on a portable black and white now everything's instant like access and sonnets color saturates the sky drops boys and girls that grow into good citizens who see something and say something or sociopaths who see something and take something I sat on a radiator vent hot ass cheeks as little links sizzled in the pan I cannot see my reflection in turbulent water so why try morning sun lights up bare branches house sidings rooftops grape arbor wrapped around top of the chain link fence Christmas tree boughs sag brittle needles litter the floor below still one mouse roaming the house won't fall for any traps if you add water to seeds they turn into something when life comes you can't reject it when death comes you can't reject it if you stop at what you do not know you are there clouds in a lens house inside rock and ice crash and clatter trash truck collectors shout go shift to low onto the next house it is natural for us to like what's similar to ourselves and to dislike what's dissimilar it is said to be a good swimmer you must forget water dropping coins in fountains does not a good swimmer make take the human form find joy there where it is Celeste's boyfriend Reed here for the New Year festivities I'm lazy since posting grades eating too much holiday food taking naps I don't need haven't had a good walk in over a week first morning 2021 brazen mouse on stove-top brew tea distant birds sing neighborhood quiet Julia Reed Molly still asleep check future forecast no snow until at least the middle of the month the tissue of existence perennially shapes itself into forms we recognize that reshape themselves into other forms the heart of the Cosmos beats beyond words thoughts and actions which are nothing more than empty show the heater blows outside's cold toes chilly understanding dwells outside words and ideas clear and muddy equal parts of primal unity you see and don't see outside ideas and words is it possible to inhabit the Tao and the mystery of things swirling in eddies of original-nature waning gibbous moon hangs over Route 2 Boston skyline appears in view Julia and I back into the city talk of religion morality Trump and the will to know why we're here two women in doctor's office tell me I must drink beer and whiskey for my test tell them I no longer drink they say it's ok for medical reasons they must run these tests then they give me questionnaire to fill out personal sex questions one asks if I am uncomfortable answering them I say no wondering if they will read my answers walking around Walden Pond in another country a group of people on horseback gallop by I narrowly escape then I see a dying horse struggling to get up off the ground I get closer and try to help someone shouts leave it alone it's not a real horse back to neighborhood walks far fewer people than in warmer weather my body warms up as I step up the pace people down the street keep chickens in the yard passing by hear the cluck-clucking past the Catholic church bells ring on the turning of the hour everything seems gray dirty houses buttoned down tight trees bare chilly air saturates the lungs mind slowly quiets aware of my breath the pace of my body methodical arm swings steady steps until nothing's left but to walk up into the sky and let things go their way take down Christmas tree remove lights garland ornaments pack them up bring to attic for another year sweep pine needles drag tree to sidewalk lined with other trees another year marked another start in the human calendar of no beginning no end it is said the longest living person ever was Peng Zu who lived for 800 years but that is nothing compared with no-time of Tao 90,000 miles is nothing measured against the limitless small minds cannot lead to great insight but merging with the limitless yields to fuller understanding work on syllabi for spring semester organize lessons no snow on the horizon new snowshoes unused corner of the room workmen continue on the house next door yet month after month nothing seems to come to completion Trump mob marches on Washington attacks and occupies Capitol building no seeming resistance encouraged by the president and his political supporters deaths on both sides the whole world watching Americans in shock knot in my stomach the entire day but who could not see this coming the past four years where to from here how move forward hatred racism misogyny xenophobia woke this morning to the words the day of night and the night of day thirty years ago this month first issue of *lift* magazine published Molly's woodblock print cover on Reeves BFK paper morning Zoom meeting with Dave talk life kids addiction recovery load of dishes dark load of clothes in washer Zoom meet with graduate student sign off on her final thesis email from Mulrooney how to teach *Spring and All* along with his new resounding long poem Boston history and geography immediately stands amongst the great Boston poems music singing unflinchingly listen to Glen Dickson's meditative music as I write layers of sound reach deep into body and mind suffusing the 10,000 things body an awakened tree mind a brilliant mirror where no dust should gather it's said a sage is never influenced by social fads or seduced by conformity things change perpetually yet return to the formless source two-hour Zoom meeting with T. J. talk poetry his new book music teaching family how recent terrorist actions in Washington not surprising a continuation of the feud old as the nation's history paddling canoes off the Gloucester shore huge wave crashes over us tossing

about in the wild water Molly says she warned us
not to go out there Molly banging computer keys
upstairs in her office working from home since
March upload syllabi for spring classes schedule lessons for first two weeks Jim posts morning photos
from Rafe's Chasm Margo Lockwood dead Margo
poet divine human being and friend Margo who I
danced with at The Midway always a laugh and a
smile her humor infectious as her wit her writing
graceful and tough first time I saw her read over
thirty years ago with Bill Corbett and Fanny Howe
old art gallery in the South End she ends one of her
poems with the line sometimes I don't realize how
Chinese I've become mother lover nourisher memoirist of the working-class experience gossip monger
extraordinaire crossing over now immortal unseasonal weather temps in the 40s all week still no
snow in the future Mitch writes he's typing up all his
poems Amanda writes about fish that can't be sold
Hinton writes that Chinese philosophy is told
through story-telling not abstract system-building
following a winding river to its source you become
bewildered walking in the sun letting your mind off
things you absorb and become absorbed this is
known as absorbing and becoming absorbed one
year ago The First Supper played its last live show at
The Midway before the pandemic shut everything
down 2 A.M. up for pee power's out house under

quiet dark shroud temperature slips down surrounding houses shady moonlight blocked by clouds no streetlights back in bed blankets tight computer lights up small area top of my hands bright as I type Trump impeached for a second time for the crime of inciting an insurrection Biden and Harris to be sworn in next week notice from my doctor I will be eligible for my virus vaccine sometime between February and April ten months since the shutdown like a long dream now reality email from the English Department am I willing to pick up a third course spring semester of course I am take trash barrels to sidewalk my poet neighbor David Blair walks past talk teaching remotely family snowshoes Zoom poetry readings reading *Billy Budd* again readying for my 6 American Authors class Frederick Douglass Herman Melville William Carlos Williams Maxine Hong Kingston Lucia Berlin Sandra Cisneros on his famous ride on a very good horse Paul Revere passing the Neck got nearly opposite where they let a charred slave's remains hang in chains living in human form never to know end trees bend in wind heavy rain water in basement spring-like temperature two young dental students at the school pull my tooth mouth numb bite down on gauze for two hours until bleeding subsides ice cream for dinner the *Lieh-tzu* says enlightened people can sense truth without going through deduction or reasoning this is known as knowing nothing yet knowing all fall from this height I might yet live give me a life without extremes to know what's enough and what isn't to slip into uncharted experience only to return and know I've been somewhere what use living one hundred years if only to see the same things come and go oh villanelle stop yelling at me to repeat lines there's no two faces alike though many people look alike like brothers and sisters but form is formless emerging and returning never the same the Way is without form take iambic pentameter please they say before the world got so small there were secrets under stones but I saw a secret in broad daylight on Mass. Ave. just the other day kids next door out to play dad shouts hey put that down put that down I said hey did you hear me put that down in 1656 she testified she'd been struck on the back with a clap of fire as her neighbor vanished in the shape of a cat aluminum ladder going up workmen chat on this MLK January holiday morning death toll over 400,000 Trump will not attend the inauguration leaving the political and social system in shambles brought America to the nadir of its existence in my lifetime everyone must die sometime end rhymes compete with the activity of Nature which never ceases Lao Tzu said a nation may have crooked leadership a destructive society or way of life but there is nothing that truth does not permeate the words

of great people must have truth a giant tree begins
as a sprout a skyscraper begins as a hole when
things reach full flourishing they begin to decline in
time I have learned how to travel extensively in
Somerville death and life are part of the same design
it's possible to stop people from going into the ocean
but impossible to stop the ocean's waves a nail driven by a hammer has no choice in the matter falling
off a ladder only one way to go smile at the sky you
just might see something you've never seen Celeste
cooks dinner roasted chickpea tomato onion and
arugula salad Tuscan white bean soup I wash pans
and help with dishes the music of the Way never
ceases tones sounds and rhythms emerge and return
its score is not scored it can be defined but not in a
fixed way say it will begin in some foreign neighborhood and where will we run when the firemen come
low and behold I hear sirens now power tools the
beeping of a backing truck restless night in and out
of sleep and dream fires water four-hundred-page
student novel I must read in one afternoon bring car
to garage some kind of leak underneath on 12 Munroe Street John Trowbridge entertained Longfellow
Stow Emerson Holmes and Whitman and later
bought a house in Arlington mindfulness is for sale
yoga is an industry let your mind roam along in the
drift of things nothing compares with simply living
out your inevitable nature this is known as simply

living out your inevitable nature syllabi posted first week lessons planned Chuang Tzu says you can't allow exterior things to penetrate your heart starts and stops occur organically like wind like trees we bend yoga is unity Tao is an ant following its path while high in the sky black holes open and close who knows as I the colonial fortifications on Central Hill Ira Thorp's dairy farm bordered by Highland and Walnut inauguration day most diverse administration in the country's history brings newfound hope for many biggest surge in pandemic due to holiday travel against all warnings in our search for joy do we find real joy two boys on basketball court mask-less bundled up bouncing basketball taking shots car repaired Joey you're set for the rest of winter Joey my mechanic says calls me Joey and prefaces and ends everything he says to me with Joey Joey how are you Joey Joey have a good day Joey Joey what can I do for you Joey reminds me of my old Italian aunts it is said only when you know what's useless can you talk of what's useful dinner of chicken cutlets noodles with butter and cheese baked zucchini for the second time in a week see poet David Blair walking in the neighborhood house behind us undergoing work on new porch house next door making progress windows and old shingles stripped replaced with new siding workmen on scaffolds shout down to man on the ground cutting the strips and sending them up on a pulley sip tea read yoga then shower I'm in Central Square talking with a woman who is a poet that I know when one by one a group of men and women gather around us it seems they are people she knows we converse for a few minutes I make to leave reaching for my cell phone only to find it is not mine and I check my other pockets each containing a cell phone but none of them mine the people in the crowd begin to claim their cell phones each time I remove one from a pocket another one is sitting in the same pocket but where is my cell phone and I realize they are playing some kind of trick on me as they begin to laugh but where is my cell phone I keep questioning the more distressed I become the more they seem to enjoy the spectacle I grow angrier and begin to smash each cell phone onto the ground then one of them slides his jacket opens and is carrying a pistol and becomes threatening what are you doing what do you want then one by one they reveal pistols and knives all I want is my cell phone I say all I want is my cell phone Zoom meeting with Michele tea and painting each of us with brand new canvas talking painting how she met Dan and how I met Molly anecdotes about Bob and what classes we will teach what colors are we using how we mix our paint grab the palette knife scoop up globs of mixed paint swirl it all over the canvas aggressively larger brush to smaller brush mix in glazing liquid two hours pass in the blink of an eye say goodbye let's do this again a bit more tweaking first painting of the year completed Celeste makes homemade individual pizzas for each of us mine with mushrooms empty the dishwasher refill it with supper dishes wash load of dark towels temperature slipping into the 20s tonight no snow in the distant forecast here where I live surrounded by many houses busy streets follow one it leads to another the new trolley Green Line gets closer each day the stop within walking distance promises rises in real estate values it is said wait before you sell your house at one time a train ran through the city before they shut it down change is what you make it thoughts arise then disappear here today gone tomorrow we only borrow them like the wild turkey on Summer Street dead and gone first week of spring classes filled to capacity do my best to encourage them to come out from behind their screens so we can see each other get to know each other make a safe community in which we can learn from each other students at various stages of pandemic fatigue burned out from remote fall semester struggling with juggling jobs family and academics American Stories 6 American Authors Introduction to Creative Writing small snow storm 3 to 4 inches on the ground just enough to shovel clear walkway down driveway out to the street clean off cars talk with neighbor will they impeach Trump when the vaccine will come hopes and fears about the new administration will Trump run again if he starts his own party it'll hurt Republicans cook supper linguine with ground turkey tomato sauce is it sauce or gravy depends on where you come from my mother and all my relatives called it gravy I mostly call it sauce rise early prep for classes set up assignments for next week green tea yoga then breakfast banana and toast what is the mystery of things how is it all woven together I miss my friends lunches together meeting for coffee rock and roll shows at the local dives hard to keep track of the days of the week as they slip in and out of each other it's been said that words impede deep insight but we look out at the world using words to point at it and we need words to communicate and make plans otherwise how do we navigate the world it's these contradictions that keep me afloat in the air I breathe if we can comprehend everything it means there's nothing left to being to understand things better look better at things you don't understand signs of the mouse again though no sightings in weeks coldest morning of the winter 7 degrees house chilly heat turned high in 1834 between Broadway and the Middlesex Canal Protestants burned down a Catholic convent no one ever held accountable plan future lessons talk with dentist arrange another tooth extraction email from my normally conservative older sister about getting rid of the crazy hate mongering politicians Trump has birthed email from doctor's office news about virus vaccine when it will be available talk of stock market crash Zoom meeting with group planning memorial for our dead friend Bob outside bright sun creates shadows an ancient wrote when matters come up one should respond beyond shadow beyond light wrong or right to write in flowery language is to hide your true intentions meter and rhyme may dance in time but sometimes hide what you need to say fuck you and the horse you rode in on is not iambic in language the Tao can become manifest best let it meander like clouds when the shroud of the pandemic lifts I want to throw a dance party cut some serious rug hug friends shout to the Cosmos loudly enough it covers its ears dream I'm in San Francisco for a writer's conference staying in an old 19th century wooden hotel sharing a room with a poet I don't know who hand-makes clothes she's making a dress in the room and reciting poems aloud downstairs in a hall writers gather some I know others I don't I jump off the wagon start drinking again out of control acting out I wake in a nice modern hotel people are telling me how crazy I was the night before insulting writers and the hotel staff nearly thrown out of the hotel when it's time to leave an angry staff member points me to a train to get to the airport but once aboard it's not the train to the airport but a train full of old rich retired senior citizens on their way to a retirement area brand new condos and buildings I'm asking for help to find the airport eventually arrive but the plane has departed I can't find my wallet or cell phone second dream in weeks where I am in San Francisco getting lost taking a train to the airport happy this morning that I did not relapse and go off the wagon big storm predicted a N'oreaster maybe a foot of snow prepare for 11 A.M. class tea yoga toast set computer up in my studio to join the class meeting why stories are important you cannot use a moonbeam to knock down a wall knowledge waits on certainty but certainty is never quite certain shovel heavy wet snow stop at intervals catch my breath heart thumping work my way slowly to end of the driveway snow turns to sleet then rain then sleet back to snow clean off cars back in the house remove wet clothes shoes and socks put on sweater with pajama bottoms teach my 11 A.M. literature class students inspired by Frederick Douglass lively compassionate group discussion back out in afternoon shovel again change and teach another vigorous discussion in creative writing class in response to in-class writing what things currently inspire you online recovery meeting more and more people each week the pandemic causing a flood of increase in drug and alcohol use new people struggling to make it through a day without using after meeting Celeste's dinner Chinese dumplings and bok choy dead mouse in the trap behind the stove a hawk a worm a mouse a thing among things our messy little house come go create dissolve appear disappear without bias even when noisy you can abide in stillness it is said you can build a wheel without spokes but you can't build a wheel with only spokes water is soft yet so strong you can strike it but it won't be injured pierce it it won't be punctured grab it but can't hold it it wears down stone and metal yet nourishes the entire world this is known as the Tao of water follow Oxford to Trull Lane Berkeley Central to Highland rows of houses brick apartments glassy storefronts signs City Hall flag flies high Somerville High School Public Library traffic cars one end to the other telephone poles streetlamps trees and down beneath it all same old earth wandering away wake at 5 A.M. attempt to rise decide to shut my eyes toss and turn until 6 drift in and out of sleep wake from dream at 8 Jim sends photos on my phone brilliant sunrise various stages over the Atlantic Independence Park in Beverly drive into the mystery the man sang get in your car and drive right on up to Beverly it is important to keep the search for the Way alive but also important never to find it overcast gray day smell snow in the air clearer to elsewhere we create our sadness and joy this passage only a temporary ride a short journey so why place so much importance on social conventions which cause daytime worries and problematic dreams at night Amanda writes she's tired of cooking the same old things during the pandemic looking for new recipes Mitch texts from Texas yesterday he was in Memphis he'll send new poems soon a student writes he's sorry to miss all the early classes and will do his best to make up the work a lone bird calls outside two short bursts at a time snow slowly starting to fall tosses about in the breeze these are the elements by which the world is modeled and formed with no purpose but a natural process of development only to rise then decline Bob and I drink at a bar not really a bar more a small convenient store cramped with a table or two they only stock top shelf hard liquor which Bob explains is why he likes it here he's thin and fit like when I met him thirty years ago calm and rational not like the Bob I knew talking about Italy and Italian activists who came to America one of them lived upstairs from the bar and the owner knew him but how could he it was too long ago brisk morning sun reflects snow 6 inches shovel driveway clean off cars back inside text Michele about dream of Bob scramble three eggs with chopped sliced turkey cup of green tea read three papers ready for 11 o'clock class first snowshoe hike of the winter azure sky trees laden down with snow around Bellevue Pond Wrights Hill reaches up to the right past the old mica mine granite walls rise straight up dressed with icicles groin muscles ache stop for drink of water talk with passing cross country skier about the Fells and the deficient forestry stunted and dying trees different kinds of winter gear mushroom foraging then off we go in different directions climb long steep hill finding my pace arms moving poles legs spread so not to trip over shoes deep steady breaths another break at the top stop to take in the surrounding landscape snow blanketed woods every direction not a human in sight loop around down Mud Trail back to the pond ducks on patches of open water legs stiff barely able to move by the time I reach the car stop at café in Medford double espresso back into Somerville slowed down by snow removal Asylum Avenue Glass House Court Jenny Lind Avenue Tube Works Court Tiger Court lost street names Celeste cooks dinner roasted red onion tomato garbanzo and kale salad lemon garlic dressing pesto toast car pulled over side of the road looks like Fanny Howe it is Fanny the car hood is up driver's door open Fanny in the driver's seat sipping a cup of tea eating a snack writing in a journal mounted on the dashboard what are you doing here she asks I ask the same question back taking a little break away from things she says not much time for writing these days so she has to make time it's an old car 1960s model light blue white trim talk about Margo how much we miss her and how we'll have a memorial reading then Ed Barrett appears but we're no longer on the side of the road but a bar it's loud no matter how hard we shout we can't hear each other Ed starts crying Fanny puts her hand on his shoulder afternoon student meeting canceled second time this week drive to the Fells to snowshoe walk part of the Skyline Trail wind penetrating cold put hood up over woolen cap steep rise up over granite hill tricky steps down over ice and rock to Molly's Spring Road across Molly's Spring to the reservoir lesser traveled trail around the shoreline eat trail lunch sitting on a boulder in a cozy cove wispy clouds lots of sunshine tree boughs laden with snow not a squirrel or chipmunk in sight no birdsongs or bird sightings except one lone chickadee bouncing on a low-hanging branch another tooth extraction at oral surgeon Dr. Onkamon fits temporary bridge take it out when you eat and sleep wash with soap and water back in two weeks for six-hour appointment to work on permanent bridge David Kirschenbaum writes would I like to send a selection images of my paintings for Boog City visual arts edition he'd like to use 10 so send 20 he will choose Somerville's forward thinking Dr. Luther V. Bell once removed a patient's crushed leg with a razor antique saw and a darning needle place wet dark load in dryer put load of whites in washer unload dishwasher scrub frying pan no sign of mice since new traps all still set in place read four student papers tea then yoga and breakfast smoothie banana blueberries strawberries and walnuts out to market groceries for dinner leftover chicken diced mixed with broccoli sauteed in garlic olive oil white wine and crushed hot pepper tossed with rigatoni Roy Orbison on the radio "Only the Lonely" stop for espresso at café damp gray day spits drizzle small alligator on trail first one ever seen walk carefully around it then large alligator I try to skirt around locks its mouth around my leg but I don't feel anything falling to the ground I begin to jam it in the eye with my walking stick harder and harder screaming each time I strike until it releases me and slithers off I run out of woods to my car shouting to people what happened and warning them not to enter the woods but they pay me no mind 6 A.M. awake internet down brew red tea first clear sunrise in days Celeste writes she won't be home until Saturday Mitch writes from L.A. the center of the manufactured illusion next stop San Francisco it's easy to talk about the wisdom of the ancients difficult to practice it once a man thought he could win a kingdom and butted his head against a mountain to move it out of his way but slipped and fell into the ocean and drowned the Way is impartial has no entrusted interests during the 17th and 18th centuries Somerville Ave. then Milk Row a trade route connecting Boston with the countryside she sits on the park bench legs crossed pink hair stares off lifts her cigarette to black lips in death we dissolve and merge with all things two hours this morning with the UMass IT Helpdesk Blackboard not sending out my class assignments first long chat exchange then long phone call clear your browser try another browser remove and install Google Chrome again if something disrupts a stream and ruins the flow the stream reverts or takes on a new form keeps on flowing Amanda writes that she absolutely loves tacos how she needs three little buttons the three little buttons she got for the task are too small Peter sends galleys of my memoir with some edit suggestions image of my painting on the cover more mice around but none going for the peanut butter in the traps time to change the bait Zoom meeting with Renata our first meeting and conversation in over a year gossip news life art writing let's do it again soon several inches snow overnight just enough to shovel clear up to end of driveway clean off cars drive to grocery store wait in line cash out forgot my wallet in my other coat at home drive back to house back to market and home again change bait in mousetraps from peanut butter to tiny hot dog pieces snow falling heavier through the day wait until it ends before I shovel again try to flush out muddy water with clear water and you churn up more dirt the Tao is best left alone you cannot improve on it what makes everything happen some people need to know that someone or something is huffing and puffing making the winds blow and the world turn hang onto those questions you will only be confused too much thinking bruises the spirit butternut squash soup for lunch bread and butter cup of tea read student memoirs send out assignments for next week's classes watch the snowflakes fall all afternoon more snow more shoveling hard at work on edits for the memoir add new material tighten down sentences read sections aloud in order to listen Miller's River long since filled in exuded noxious gasses while low tide flats exposed decomposing animal waste from slaughterhouses and sausage factories along the shore come go create dissolve appear disappear inhale exhale spirit and body merge with the natural rise and fall of energy new file from Hugh for the next song that we will record upload it into GarageBand practice guitar parts rhythm solo fills and finally vocals rise early read and grade eight student quizzes thirteen more to go tea yoga breakfast banana cranberry bread toasted ready for 11 A.M. class Amanda writes that this little piggy went to a new home today Peter

writes that everything tastes like salt it is said that
once a man wandered as if lost in a wilderness
beyond the dust of this world with no duties to per-
form another man wore his knowledge like a piece
of jewelry to appear enlightened as if he held the
sun and moon in his hands every morning slam
bangs of planks power tools delivery trucks shouts
in Spanish over the noise month after month and
the house next door still not complete Celeste roasts
vegetables spread hummus on rollups fill with veg-
etables and feta cheese these are the moments easi-
ly forgotten over a half million pandemic deaths
across the country still not one vaccine appointment
available in the entire state governor says we must
wait not enough vaccines to go around two chicka-
dees bathing in the melted planter water splashing
flap wings submerged completely chirping celebrat-
ing this sunny warm winter day early settlers discov-
ered at least seven streams with origins in the Mystic
River now new condos rise everywhere with million
dollar price tags in my childhood people called
Somerville Slummerville a relative once asked me
you're going to move there Gerrit's birthday I think
I heard him calling to the birds at sunrise still no
word on the vaccine availability though promises
it's on the way finish reading student quizzes for
one class onto essays for another what are the key
turning points in the Frederick Douglass book that

led to his escape from slavery atop Cobble Hill property values rose as they pushed back and crowded out entirely the pigpen neighborhoods below awake before the sunrise brew tea watch Glenn Dickson solo performance allow it to wash over me like the dawning of the new day suddenly birds outside begin to respond to Glenn's call become one all things connected six-hour dentist appointment three sets of Novocain injections ground four teeth to fit the new bridge jaw sore gums raw and tender throbbing headache soup for supper ice cream dessert first virus vaccine shot scheduled for Thursday restrictions being lifted around the state accompanied by a rise of infections I don't want a fancy car a big house a flock of disciples I have enough to think about enough to see enough to hear today and tomorrow the same last year this year no change trying to become enlightened is easy ending delusions is hard ice melts but the sky says snow who knows how many breaths are left before we let go Amanda sings about a fox in the snow and a girl in the snow and a boy on a bike and a kid in the snow what do they know make the most of it while you can haircut goatee trim clear morning sunlight through windowpane falls on flowers atop table across wooden floor heavy winds during the night continue last year's leaves still blow off trees gutters rattle I shudder to think about all the Chinese people being attacked ignorance and hatred a way of life it's hard not to mind how others act on this very day in 1955 a black schoolgirl Claudette Colvin refused to give up her bus seat for a white person arrested and charged with multiple offenses people busy day and night to achieve goals heads aswirl busy all their lives unaware how fast the breath of existence fades how trying to find what's real becomes more distant the ups and downs of the world weigh heavy upon us it is said that grinding a brick on a rock is a waste upload new guitar tracks into band folder marinate steaks in wine onions and garlic before broiling saute asparagus with butter shallots and white wine over noodles wait in huge room until 9:45 appointments called to check in line sanitize hands put on new mask move slowly safe distance answer questions receive paperwork sit in chair in another big room as vaccinators walk up and down the aisles to give shots Johnson & Johnson only one shot required wait fifteen minutes in case of a reaction watch for side effects next two days sun bright chilly late afternoon walk up and over the hill more and more traffic fewer people out walking far off horn of commuter rail taking workers back out to the suburbs and home for a meal and a night's rest to return again tomorrow morning we bloom and fade like flowers gather and disperse like clouds I wish I could see through worldly concerns but worry burns won't set me free read student short stories explosions reform school rape futuristic worlds seeing life with a new eye working in a coffee shop unable to speak English drill sergeants military training lost love dead parents drug addiction dead cats trunk in a secret room contains a severed hand detective tracking serial killers coming out to parents teenage pregnancy don't go down to the basement despite their dislike of dangerous places people are always fooled into going what's gone is gone what hasn't come needs no thought a lot of what passes for success is merely bondage and chains loss and gain delusions Jim posts a photo of The Cut in Gloucester last time there before recovery Gerrit drops THC tincture on my tongue when I arrive at his house says let's go for a ride he drives us around town our eyes aglow smiles on our faces says let's go to The Cut we walk out towards the lighthouse my leg slips between a gap in the granite slabs bruised and bloody I still have the scars Amy Winehouse is at the club where my band is playing but we are having equipment problems and can't get the sound to come out Amy approaches the stage says there's some kind of electrical short in the wiring but we don't have a way to repair it I ask what are you doing here she answers that once before anyone knew her she sang here I tell her she is very beautiful and she kisses me on the cheek and Levi says she's is not Amy Winehouse but she looks like her after 18,000 years elapsed Pang died his breath became wind mist and clouds his voice thunder his left eye the sun his right eye the moon his head the mountains his blood rivers his muscles fertile land his facial hairs the stars and Milky Way his fur forests his bones valuable minerals his bone marrow sacred diamonds his sweat rain and the fleas on his fur carried away by wind became animals spring-like day temps hit 60 folks out in shorts and t-shirts bike path overrun walkers bikers joggers parents with strollers folks sit on porches sip drinks speaking stories of our lives thoughts feelings endeavors concerns aspirations the very definitions of what we are as if we were the center of identities we assume ourselves to be dear Tao that nestles the ten thousand things into a single living tissue please shine the path of light that stretches across the darkness carries with it our deeply felt human experiences until everything opens away as it does drive to Bob's for chicken cutlets then to market for vegetables and fruit jazz on the radio "Monk's Dream" oversize hawk circles air pockets against sunset pink feathered clouds shifts in currents adapts second by second to changes the Tao in motion the activity of Nature never ceases snow melt bodies writhe and coil in water rushing down the street into the sewer and to the sea final changes in new book off to publisher one year ago UMass Boston closed because of pandemic two weeks' time to return and teach online official email claims we might be back on campus this fall young woman in market looks at me I turn my head away finish checking out groceries she looks again I turn my eyes away uneasy she approaches maybe I know her and can't tell because of her mask she says something I can't understand I ask her what she said she repeats louder I like your outfit perhaps this is some kind of joke I am wearing my beat-up overalls and a jeans jacket are you kidding I ask no she says you look really cool I look like an old man who needs a new outfit I tell her no no no she says you look really cool the mice eat baits from traps without triggering them not so dumb these little creatures tiny buds appear on branches dance in the warm breeze from these preludes to spring hope springs seasons slide into each other changes come and go before you even know an end clocks turned ahead for spring mornings dark evenings light but the Tao knows no time past present future one continuum the moon slides across the sky wind blows through trees moonlight and wind sounds wear away layer after layer temps drop back down this morning 18 degrees feels like 6 with wind why can't I forget my worries accept the world of dust everything we know and see will vanish sooner or later there's no need to arrange a thing body is a bubble lasts 'til bursting sound of metal crashing and bouncing smoking car upside down side of the road hissing noises electric sparks people inside I shout get out get out of the car repeat get out get out of the car walk closer but fear an explosion four bodies upside down a man looks out let's get out let's get out they slowly climb through broken windows shattered glass everywhere battered and beaten one left inside isn't moving he's gone one man yells leave him I'm dialing 911 on my cell the same man screams at me to drop my phone he has a gun take him out take him out another man yells I turn and run for woods on the side of the road shot fired behind me a bullet whistles by strikes a tree get him get him get him I hear another shot misses into the trees run for my life and crouch behind a boulder rid of the bondage the depression I know ends when young I drank to mourn the ways of the world but that's wasted effort now I see clearly the ways of the world in morning radiance outside my window birds celebrate feel freed from my shackles leave the tangles behind the eyes reach beyond what ruins our lives one year a thousand years distance upon distance how can it be any less sitting on the sofa wrapped in wool blanket the heat clicks on new day old day same day sometimes I think I have traveled extensively in Somerville other times I think I have not yet begun to travel a few words can channel the universe from the sky turn it to dust gathers on the windowsill Amanda Zoom performance plays ukulele sings drinks shots of whiskey says who drinks brandy when you have whiskey clicks an old fashioned typewriter for rhythm I write Facebook comment Amanda is divine variation of the dream again out of town some literary event staying at a hotel time to return home but can't get to the airport unable to pack my bags too many clothes more I pack the more clothes appear Molly says I must have some kind of fear of being far away in strange surroundings another three-hour session at the dentist filing front teeth taking impression for permanent bridge on Prospect Hill the first flag ever raised against the British where cattle grazed the Great Pasture now children play under masked parents' watchful eyes temps warming again sunny days people refuse vaccines others seem to think everything is back to normal businesses reopen traffic increasing others cry the pandemic is a hoax most mornings I try to return to sleep but unable I wake make tea read the house quiet Jim posts views of the ocean texts that Wieners is receiving more attention than ever too bad it didn't come when he was alive Michele sends video her talk on music for justice in preparation for her visit to my American Stories class times differ but stories remain the same how to know what's true what's platitude what's affectation she writes there's sleeve flapping in the night sky inside a hand that manipulates stars turns them on and off I no longer fill my cup and toast the wine gods when gloom comes I wait until it disappears as the story of our lives opens away yet we cannot leave the world's tangles behind remind me again about forms of poetry we force words into cages or cells until wild joy no longer wanders boundless and free how did someone like me get here how to see through this mess first t-shirt walk of the year sun warm on my shoulders parents push baby strollers cyclists joggers dog walkers folks gather on lawns in backyards front and back porches smell food on grills pot smoke in the air music voices who thew the Frisbee onto the street back home cook turkey meatloaf noodles and broccoli darkness falls later each evening another day drifting in this life no origin no end these words of mine drift and scatter with the ten thousand things more shootings more killings week in week out headlines pass like water forgotten quickly as they flash thoughts and prayers won't change a thing lip service is all some people hate six days a week only to pray to Jesus on the seventh if Jesus walked amongst us he'd be hated by the haters sooner or later something's got to give but for now hammers bang low clouds hang the morning bird that sang yesterday nowhere around the business of poetry makes me cringe it is said toxins are made from a pot full of bugs I remember inkwells in school desks I urge my students write your poem drafts with pencils in notebooks connect body spirit mind breath don't worry about misspellings typos bad grammar wrong words or saying the wrong thing I hear a workman sing and whistle all heart spacious and free the comings and goings of the day blossom then fade away stir change never the same always the same if you reach out to touch stars you startle a millennium Ed writes that the lockdown has seen him put together two new manuscripts he and Jennie will spend the summer in Ireland long as they are allowed in and what changes online teaching has brought condo conversion every which way in this city buy the old gut 'em out strip down to stud build 'em new and mark 'em up Mitch writes he's back in Texas over a month on the road new poems in loads next stop Zen retreat walking in woods along wide trails and over granite knobs to fast-running stream slip on rocks fall into deep pool fully clothed treading water struggle to climb out people above extend hands down to help but can't reach pull myself up inch by inch on the ground to catch my breath clothes wet suddenly large mushrooms size of spaghetti pots fall from trees never seen any like these wonder are they edible pick one up with my two hands to carry it home plumber phones with estimate to replace the faucet and dishwasher wow that much drizzle wind raw temps never count your spring before it is hatched my travel along the Way is just now beginning a distant church bell marks the time I look out the window and a red cardinal flies across the neighbor's yard leaves no tracks drops onto a branch followed by its partner here I am amongst tens of thousands in the city keeping social distances as the pandemic continues to kill people still refuse vaccines there are no shortcuts in the way of the Tao lost count of all the markers I've passed farther and farther from where I started yet no closer to the realm beyond sun and moon opposite side of sky no matter how hard I try I'm the same evening breeze though screens in open living room windows birds sing celebratory songs long ago it was written those who know don't speak those who speak don't know Chinese translation via email from student lovers on opposite ends of the Yangtze River drinking from the same water sparrow fixed statue-like on peak of neighbor's roof heat on first time in days some mornings contentment comes in the midst of everything never remains long enough to share a meal leaves me saddened nothing had been done during our visit I need to lose my accumulated possessions too much stuff not enough room and use for it all what good thousands of books clothes I will never wear musical instruments dozens and dozens of paintings stacked up boxes and boxes of papers letters poems and story drafts who will look after it all when I am gone which won't be long we hurry back from where we set out this is known as hurrying back from where we set out in ancient times there were those who gave up learning to master the art of the Tao they were known as those who give up learning here where I live houses on the left houses on the right houses in front and behind dwellings fashioned true cars come and go people come and go no one thing or action the same 1843 a surveyor plots the first choice section in what becomes known as Spring Hill one of the city's seven hills looking through death dark and light call you by the new name no-name wild joy boundless free look too closely vision blurs nothing to be seen listen closely ears go numb nothing to be heard the flow of energy rises ever upward Gerrit lives among the stars leaving the human crowd behind he visits us in unseen dazzling excellence having left the dust for greater purity says the Tao is so small it contains nothing inside it yet big enough it has no bounds I await the passing seasons aware my essence will fade all too soon clinging to passing clouds floating with them in grand procession while roads stretch far off in all directions yet never reach beyond the world Michele guest in the American Stories class stories as songs discuss immigration English as a second language class pandemic the American Dream she and Dan sing and play songs together he guitar she flute internet down again regular thing these days roast red peppers broiled chicken mashed potatoes 6:41 in the evening still light out John posts photo of Gabe reading a poem in Gerrit's solarium blue jay bounces on the porch railing in the pouring rain neighbor's dogs bark up a frenzy at their back door want back in the energy throughout our bodies is a complete network oblivion is difficult to imagine this is known as trying to imagine oblivion is difficult MFA student theses readings today poets fiction writers ready to graduate and go out into the world more writers more degrees does the world need more writers I can't help but wonder where will all the words go whirling around the endless landscape of eternity oh sun oh moon that shine on this earth teach me to stop wallowing in ignorance liberate me so I might begin the path of the long ascent Julia calls can I drive her to the homemade pasta store she's making a Bolognese sauce buys linguine mafalde and gnocchi I'll put some in the freezer she says load of towels in the washer water in the basement boxes in the living room up to the attic read student poems and Bartleby essays I too prefer not to too but trapped like Nippers Turkey Ginger Nuts and the narrator vacuum floors clear clutter in kitchen and living room prep for Julia's twenty-fifth birthday celebration falafel tzatziki lentil soup Greek salad Greek meatballs pita bread baklava cookies and cheesecake I write to John about my dream pedaling to Gloucester to visit him on an old-fashioned three-wheeled tricycle in the blackest of nights when I reach Stage Fort Park giant sky-high ice blocks cover the harbor crashing over the park and Western Ave. I turn around in terror fearing I'll be crushed pedal madly away John writes the ice blocks are the ones who name label and identify the howling void thereby making real only their story and that my bike is the vehicle of anarchy that saved me my escort through paradise I'm lucky to have been inoculated in my youth with some Frank Zappa serum of the present-day composer who refuses to die Jim writes he hates National Poetry Month I write back I do too John writes that poets are on the loose and the authorities will round up the usual suspects send out vocal track Hugh returns the latest mix guitar tracks for two more songs followed by vocals looking to get the demo ready by late spring as back-up I facilitate the recovery meeting since our regular facilitator is having computer problems five years a member of this group this the most stressful demanding academic year ever students feel it too tired punch-drunk from the technology and confining Zoom classes everyone eager to return to campus next fall early morning stand on the porch soak up sun warm breeze easy on the bones read and grade student papers write to Michele and Dan about how much I enjoy their record layered string textures intermittent flute sweet vocal harmonies and the breadth of emotion in the various songs tea yoga even when not thinking there is thought geese have settled permanently in Boston no longer fly north and south with the seasons shifting climate the reason some say the Earth is flat imagine that the states with the least amount of vaccinated people are the ones with the highest pandemic rates some say they need their guns for when Antifa comes ready for 11 A.M. American Stories class today paintings as stories narratives in Jacob Lawrence migration series and Edward Hopper what do they say about us and the American experience it is said Tao brought forth the one the one brought forth more and the more brought forth myriad things t-shirt walk bright sun run in to neighbor poet David Blair returning from his walk talk walks virus vaccine teaching fatigue poetry Bernadette Mayer's sublime *Midwinter Day* stop and talk with neighbor Marcia how's the girls how's your son how's your mother thirteen day care kids wrists tied to a rope led across the street sun hot on my arms and neck people out and about the man in the butcher shop has a lamb carcass up on his cutting table bring my guitars to the shop for set-ups record lead tracks for "Hurry Hurry" then glitch with GarageBand email Levi who replies and helps me solve the problem cook pasta with tuna for me and Celeste one of her favorites she just secured job as a research engineer broil steak for Molly wash dishes and scrub pans it is said nothing in life is better than being free but free from what when and where there are no untroubled days in my life freedom is a distant rolling cloud but you can't reach out and grab it in Zen the transition from bondage to freedom is described as melting or unlocking sometimes I wonder how many more days in this life sometimes I am a dancer sometimes I am a dunce once I was a snake winding my way today my teeth ache my shoulder aches my breath is not as strong is in my youth my hair and beard gray my flesh droops my skin often itches sit outside the café at a table sip espresso watch cars and people pass an old woman says you look comfortable I tell her I am stop at pharmacy pick up scripts go to bank for cash gas up car pick guitars up from shop stop at market beside littered tracks overgrown weeds toppled shopping carts junk tires trash graffiti redbrick backside of old Derby Desk Factory two men in café talk Trump the election's stolen they have proof showed on Fox News how he was tried twice for the same crime and found innocent each time what's wrong with people in this country there's some kind of plot to steal the country and no one is paying any attention another one looks at me and asks what do you think young black man shot by a cop trial of Chauvin what if he gets off class discussion of Baldwin's "Notes of a Native Son" students talk about Harlem riot and how the same things are happening now polish the mind each day don't allow dust to gather it is said the ancient sages used their minds like pure mirrors welcoming nothing refusing nothing reflecting everything holding nothing living perfectly empty perhaps now that the weather is warming the mice will leave the house Celeste saw a mouse in her room last night caught two in traps in the last week handwritten letter from Carol white paper pink ink with a poem and two photos of me and Julia attending a reading she gave in 2012 three weeks to the end of the semester fewer and fewer students showing up for class one student who hasn't appeared in three weeks and is behind on assignments writes that she needs to pass the class in order to graduate nothing compares with living out our inevitable natures but nothing is more difficult than that new construction on the house behind us tearing down walls in second floor throwing out wreckage out windows into dumpster in driveway Celeste texts that today is ticket day 7 A.M. move the car to School Street before ticket person arrives what use street cleaning the street is never really clean April 16 9

A.M. rain turns to heavy snow coming down hard and fast sip green tea read student honors manuscript in fiction heat comes on spring tease gone Zoom coffee meeting with Dave talk recovery talk our fathers talk raising children writing music sleep patterns recording guitar tracks phone call with Carol talk her book she's been putting together for six years and Julia and Celeste she can never remember Celeste's name vaccine shots and being stuck indoors for a year and Gerrit and what do I think of his ideas about the inanimate we agree he believed they are living essences and Olson's lines I wake you stone love this man which she writes into her notebook always writing everything into her notebooks yes yes she says yes love this man hike west side Walden Pond down to Great Meadow Swamp along the edge beaver wreaking havoc with trees in various stages coming down pass a family who warn of ticks along the trail climb backside of Emerson's Ridge atop the lookout views in all directions rolling into distances sit on flat granite boulder for rest gather it all in thoughts fading to their source sometimes for a brief moment everything is open to me trees brush granite stretching away snack and water mix of sun and clouds black flies menacing whenever the breeze stops slowly make my way back down steep off trail right leg slips into blind hole between two boulders struggle to lift myself out lucky no

damage back onto main trail closer to the pond
crowds of people coming and going in all directions
back home the walk held in my mind shines bright
this morning clear sky buds swell others break into
bloom sip tea on front porch read *Woman Warrior*
by Maxine Hong Kingston for 6 American Authors
class birds form a choir temp nearing 70 back inside
load of dishes in washer yoga followed by banana
and raisin toast shower prepare for 11 o'clock class
watch videos of various dancing performances student
says she never considered dance as a way of
telling stories summer temps yield to thunderstorms
and heavy wind then a drop down to 40s this morning
heat back on Li Po's "The River-Merchant's Wife:
A Letter" discuss imagery persona and epistolary
poetry and how you can write a love poem without
using the word love assign students to write their
own letter poems like a river start small become
large why cling to traditions of past generations it is
said sages adapt to changing times take appropriate
measures to see what new forms form when things
reach full flourishing they begin to decline new construction
every turn detours traffic backups heavy
machinery racket yellow vested tradesmen and the
cop waves me through Bread and Roses Strike of
1912 for American Stories class Levi and Hugh write
first vaccine shots perhaps there is live rock and roll
in our future Julia texts she'll come for dinner Friday

night would I cook fish and a friend has lost a son to a drug overdose Chauvin found guilty on three counts but don't hold your breath for real change sixteen-year-old black girl shot and killed by cops very night of the verdict and a black man shot and killed by cops very next day will America ever be great how long must we wait dinner at the Corbett home with Bill and Beverly remark this could be the first time ever I am the only guest for dinner drink lots of wine first time in many years I've had a drink Bill remarks better here than anywhere Beverly pulls me aside and says that I should be careful around Bill now that he is sick my book on Pressed Wafer probably won't be published I pretend I don't know how sick Bill is he returns from upstairs with a painting for me I know you have always liked this he says I want you to have it Beverly asks is he sure he wants to give that away now he tells her Beverly this painting is meant for Joe Beverly and I walk the dog she holds my arm like she always has when we walk the dog we are in New York and she says she never liked Boston and this is a good place for William to be now I start to cry about Bill she smiles kisses me on the cheek says I know I know bottles and cans crash and clank swollen trash bags packed on shopping cart sings his way out of nowhere read proofs from Boog City feature interview selection from forthcoming memoir this new long poem and paintings stop at Bob's on way home from translating with her lamb tip dinner chef's salad for Molly nine people shot by cops since Chauvin conviction seems like cops' revenge new guitar files uploaded into The First Supper demo folder cold rainy morning dogwood tree in the neighbor's yard blooms yellow flowers Molly's tulips bursting forth in planters on the front porch tomato pepper and herb seedlings sprout under grow lamps no sign of a mouse in nearly two weeks Julia comes for dinner baked halibut mashed potatoes broccoli cake for dessert talk politics movies jobs Celeste's upcoming graduation ceremony it's snowing magnolia petals and a violin strings tuned to evening those who let go of the Way and trust only in intelligence are in peril life given in spring is taken back in autumn words can be troublesome it starts with the tongue once you speak inappropriately nothing can undo your words I walked a mile in another's shoes and got a blister mister can you show me where the end-rhyme goes when wind blows it away today I will read student poems wash a load of white clothes continue cleaning the kitchen cabinets cook pasta with chicken and broccoli do yoga and wait for the Great Clod to show me the way to show me the way the search for right is not the same as the search for truth one hour twenty minutes to drive twenty-one miles to Weymouth traffic back to pre-pandemic madness crawl through the O'Neill Tunnel all the way through Boston to the south shore memorial service son of dear friend thought of one of my children dying before me too much to bear grade student quizzes count down days to semester's end when will the weather break day after day gray cool temps on and off rain yet flowers bloom birds continue to sing Molly's herbs under grow lights rise straight in 1656 a local woman testified she'd been struck on the back with a clap of fire as her neighbor vanished in the shape of a cat and that was that the stories we hear like the midnight ride of Paul Revere not what they seem he never made it far as Longfellow proclaims a guitar does not make sound but its strings resound through it strings must have a balance of tight and loose in order to play the tune it is said we depend on life temporarily and death is where we ultimately return birth is an act of the Way death is the transformation of things bring me the right words so that I might place them in the right order the mind the master of form iambic be scorned and stop messing my heart around let the nature of the poem find what suits it Jim writes that her poems are sounds from heaven and Gerrit is the mother of us all Fanny writes she's leaving Boston moving to California to be closer to her family Mitch writes that he's back in Boston we will meet up soon Ed writes he loves when I write about food sends his new manuscript the insurance company writes a letter we are behind on payments for a policy we terminated months ago poetry constrained by rules can be like trying to put a square peg in a round hole why should the world have permanently fixed laws they should be adjusted to the times and the mores of the people this morning I invite clear sky for company and try to find words to converse but there is no dialogue with empty sky free and going on without end to trust old age is to descend into that sky alone this is known as trusting old age and descending into the sky alone Jim writes that he is on his way to a bird sanctuary on the Ipswich River the young couple on the second floor of the three decker next door are moving for the past week they have been filling up their small car daily with all their personal belongings and one trip at a time taking everything elsewhere the family who live on the second floor on the other side are having a party Spanish music fills the air along with the aroma of grilling meat drinking beer talking loudly children and adults alike Celeste home from staying at her boyfriend's grilled cheese on sourdough bread with tomato soup final papers drop in from 6 American Authors course on Sandra Cisneros Hugh drops final mixes of The First Supper's eleven-song Pandemic Demos Celeste cooks Vietnamese chicken soup with rice scallions parsley and lime party at

Jack Kerouac's family home in Lowell full of relatives that I don't know Jack thin young bright blue eyes blaze drinking nips one after another people telling him slow down don't drink so much he pays them no mind seems to enjoy their warnings we talk about writing and *Time Being* I tell him I couldn't have done it without him he laughs unscrews the cap of another nip and downs it in one gulp have something to eat Jackie his mother says I tell Memere I know her from Jack's books chilly dark rainy morning last week of classes emails from students ask extensions for their papers Amanda sings Billy don't take your guns to town John sings kiss kiss bang bang all this coming and going where do we ever end up Jim writes as things seem to get back to normal he feels strangely isolated walking eight or nine miles a day in woods along rivers amongst wild creatures that inhabit them he walks away from this unnamed feeling but the more he walks the more it follows and how Koko has reached the end of his journey time to put his spirit brother down searching for Gerrit Lansing I set out among fast-forming clouds moving quickly across blue sky the earth below falls away my eyes reach beyond what ruins our lives enter a deep state amongst all the distance who is it taught me to fly wingless carrying swarming thoughts there is no original home where go to from here never to rest the mind unfurls like clouds' perpetual motion to who knows where in perfect clarity surely spirits from the past roam here long ago I must have traveled in search of the Way looking for the old master finding empty sky drifting drifting beyond life and death to catch a glimpse of him simply the twist of a cloud coming and going as I turn and descend homeward to my sofa and tea words phrases and things I wish would go away mindfulness you got this wellness you killed it be in the moment you need to love yourself before you can love anyone else just keep positive thoughts a lot of this you brought on yourself eat healthy everything happens for a reason just sayin' my bad chill out TGIF yeah no work hard play hard personal fitness coaches personal trainers Zoom poetry readings on sale now Throwback Thursday Facebook Memories "Jumping Jack Flash" "Stairway to Heaven" selfies sushi bad pizza thank god thoughts and prayers are with you and last though not least The East Bumfuck Annual Poetry Prize Nick from the Midway writes they're planning to open full capacity in the fall bands with shows canceled last year will have first option do we want to reschedule bring Celeste's car into shop for service power went out some time during the night back on but internet down now no access to student writing it is said that rubbing the skin makes old people feel better settling the heart eases stress what creates things is formless and if you abandon the things of the world your form will be unbound why strive for reputation and fame in fifty years you'll be no different from anybody else weed the garden uproot the knotweed fill paper yard waste bags to the brim good to soil the hands the ground from which everything is born returns us to the origin more people vaccinated fewer people wearing masks outdoors it is said a whale out of water will be overrun by ants hike Julia's Loop Trail trees and plants gold green nearing full spring bloom chorus of bird songs mosquitoes kept in check by a medium breeze up the granite hill to the top knob stop for water and snack look out over forest stretching down and out on all sides descend back down two trail bikers pass with a nod trees waver in wind big old white pine creaks the forms of Nature swell and deflate deer tracks around vernal pool wood pecker chips away steady beat across the woods the activity of Nature does not cease it does not write iambs and trochees it does not make end rhyme or enter poetry contests it does not point out the secret within the secret the white of the moon is the light of the sun this is known as the light of the sun is the white of the moon the Tao starts with water flow endlessly it is there when the wind rises when clouds gather when thunder rumbles and lightning strikes when rain falls ungraspable undefinable give it a name it's the wrong name roast chicken with fresh herbs garlic and white wine sour cream and chive mashed potatoes broccoli sauteed in olive oil garlic and hot pepper flakes how can I stop calling attention to the faults of others falling off a high horse hurts though not everyone vaccinated the governor intends to open everything up for Memorial Day weekend no masks indoors or outdoors let the Red Sox pack the fans once again into Fenway Park the workers building the new stairway on the house behind have returned the third time they have put in the stairs and then removed them the woman who owns the condo keeps complaining no more money until the job's done right I hear her say arrive in the world without baggage leave without baggage this is known as being unencumbered knowing a lot of information is not wisdom dear professor is there anything that can be done for the student in question she's had technical trouble this semester dear academic support the student in question missed 2/3rds of the classes never turned in one assignment the semester's now over why didn't she reach out earlier we could have put some kind of plan in place we live in a world of rules and regulations designed to beat down our inner nature when we tax our inner nature we stray from the Way and lose clarity I would rather have friends than own the world Celeste tries on her graduation dress Molly takes measurements for alterations

where there is hidden there is found where there is
bound there is freed where there is birth there is
death where there is sky there is earth where there
is firm there is soft where there is society there is
conform where birds sing the Tao reminds of things
not understood this is known as not understanding
Mitch leaves a message he's back in town hanging
down by the river on Memorial Drive he just left the
Raven Bookstore talking with some guy about anarchism tomorrow in New York for his sister's graduation let's hang out in the next couple of weeks drop
Molly's car off in shop 10 A.M. Brookline appointment with my psychiatrist back in Boston for 1 P.M.
appointment with dentist finally able to complete
the impression first day of air conditioner use I complain I'm too cold Molly complains she's too hot first
light of sun reflects off neighbor's yellow house
empty clean dishes from dishwasher fill with dirty
drink tea listen the birds and the temporary quiet
before the city day sounds emerge and one by one
the bangs clangs cars trucks voices kid shouts dog
barks jet planes train whistles and the high spark of
the day firing on all cylinders Mass. Pike all the way
out through the Berkshires into New York up to
Troy Staybridge Suites Hotel Celeste's graduation
from Rensselaer ceremony four hours long Dr. Fauci
guest speaker lunch with Celeste's boyfriend's family who say grace thanking God for Celeste's and her

boyfriend's college success and for the food you think god could have done a little better than burgers and dogs dinner at our favorite Italian restaurant in the area pasta calamari eggplant homemade burrata porchetta veal with figs grilled salmon back to the hotel Celeste and Julia share their own room three police cruisers on hand disturbance amongst some hotel guests people yelling in the lobby sleep deep wake to view of distant hills breakfast and drive home back through the Berkshires Springfield Worcester into the city rise early post final grades yoga tea and toast right now I'm writing a right-now line about Molly's perennials bursting forth on the front porch and front patio how the temperature dropped twenty degrees since yesterday while the sun climbs higher into the late morning sky thoughts arise then disappear here where I live paved roads crowded houses streets lined with parked cars telephone poles connected by lines stretch out far as the eye can see squirrels rats birds of prey small birds rabbits raccoons under the same sun and moon watches over the great wildernesses of the world life unfurls and retracts as things of the Cosmos interact in the light of day and dark of night Jim calls went fishing at Rafe's Chasm after he left two men got swept into the ocean both rescued the sea takes and the sea gives back go to bank take out cash stop by café for an espresso sit outside on Main

Street watching the human flow pass by drop by market for staples fruit bread salad makings for big dinner salad for supper on the way home Archie Shepp with Sun Ra on the radio sit remain in the car listening until the song is finished write a congratulations to Amanda upon completing her college work physicist Carlo Rovelli says it's best to forget about the idea that there is spatial time at all when and how does one event end and another begin is the poem really finished at the end of the last line or is it the beginning of the next poem or all one poem continuum is it better to move free without three months ago or one night last year or this morning or next month at the end of the second week or a sneak peek into the future sooner or later turn once upon a time let go the line little league baseball team practice Trum Field on Broadway charge with a leg nearly severed straight into enemy fire then die they'll name a sports field after you detours reroute traffic all around the city to continue at least through next year major infrastructure work Celeste's second vaccine down with fever headache and chills begin summer reading Orwell's *Animal Farm* prepare for fall courses short novel biography and autobiography load of towels in washer clean kitchen floor unload clean dishes from washer turkey meatloaf brown rice and broccoli sauteed with olive oil garlic and white wine the sage lets the delusions of life go all so-called understanding and insight so that slowly the simplicity of occurrence appears of itself this is known as letting all understanding and insight go Zoom poetry reading T.J. reads full energy music attention to the nuances of each word and sound softly gently angry forceful the music like long saxophone solos sings the joy and pain of experience some things you cannot force once a flower's past its peak it's too late to look at the blossom so live on what life brings it's good to have a garden nearby cold rainy windy Memorial Day weekend Jim texts photos his first striper of the season first band show after the pandemic we've changed our entire sound all new songs setting up on stage I brought my Gibson SG instead of Fender Telecaster I tell Levi I don't have a Gibson SG anymore but he says that's the sound we need for the new songs it's just the two of us where's Hugh we're a duo now Levi says I don't know any of the songs on the set list just follow me you'll remember them once we begin Molly's gardening plans rained out for three days heat went on during the night temperature down into the 40s old interview with Joey Ramone who says there's always going to be Vanilla Ice just hope that you're smart enough to go and see The Ramones restring the Martin acoustic haven't played it for many months fingertips soft quickly sore and tender prepare new syllabus and lessons for summer course begins next week enrolled students email with questions no there are no texts required I will supply all the files and links you need yes I will allow you to do makeup work for the two classes you will miss when you are away with the National Guard attached you will find all the technical information you need to take this course online yes you are required to attend the Zoom meetings class participation and attendance are essential to your success the activity of teaching never ceases Jim writes this morning he wiped out on a loose boulder at Rafe's Chasm feels like someone dropped an anvil on his shoulder set up Zoom meetings for the summer course post first assignment finish *Animal Farm* onto *Passing* by Nella Larsen begin long slow clean up and organizing of my studio shelf books toss all unnecessary papers in trash books used courses into one big plastic crate it is said that followers of Confucius like followers of religion are involved in the world to conform in terms of government social familial moral political linguistic while Taoists don't correspond with patterns of formality the universe is an organism with no controlling center interrelated components none able to exist without the other it's not a matter of cause and effect but opposites coexisting how foolish of humans to think we can alter the course of nature work out in yard pick up yard waste from around the house and bag it work up a sweat and heavy breath Thinley drops by to take a look at the outside painting we need done my Aunt Josie dead the last of all my aunts and uncles on both sides of the family drive to Medford for the service greet her three children and other cousins barely recognizable the occasional remember this or that decades and decades no contact nothing in common small groups of old timers gather in corners talk softly in Italian my aunt's cold shriveled body in the open casket surrounded by flowers and Christian symbols angels crosses the Virgin Mary the Infant of Prague it is said the more liberty and love you give the more you allow things in yourself to take place Celeste and I drive to Revere Beach walk along the Boulevard intense heat beach crowded this Sunday afternoon families teenagers kite flyers water icy though bathers brave it smell of weed permeates the air along with various food smells fried fish clams French fries burgers dogs long lines at Kelley's Famous Roast Beef cars and motorcycles up and down the strip music blasting we lament the disappearance of Bianchi's Pizza where she and Julia and I would stop for a slice and I stopped for a slice nearly half a century ago with teenage friends building recently demolished along with the rest of the block new condo under construction rises to the sky concrete condos far as the eyes can see in both directions where once an amusement park and food kiosks and a famous roller coaster ruled the whirling sound of the speeding cars up down and around the tracks the shrieks of riders back home Celeste cooks dinner of lemon chicken and rice with spinach guy on YouTube says he can't wait to tell me exactly who I must become some people got all the nerve three days in a row temps rise to the high 90s weather people say could be the hottest days of the summer man is an integral part of Nature not here to dominate it the barber pole appears to go up and down but does it really or only giving the appearance a pebble tossed into the water drops straight down gives the illusion of extending outward on the surface thought after thought after thought without hesitation the consciousness streams no real meaning but senseless present moments this the totality of Tao act in accordance to the pattern of things that exist don't oppose it an interdependence of everything mutually arises and falls not forced or unduly self-conscious forms appear to us as some kind of order like grain in wood water patterns or markings in stone yet there is no obvious order this is known as Li when you fly in dream you are flying when you scream in dream you become choked up rushing through some kind of big shipping harbor huge ocean going ships being loaded and unloaded metal boxes lifted and stacked by long-necked cranes I'm trying to locate a specific box asking questions to various workmen the location of the box I am seeking out each pointing me in a new direction up and down rows and rows of stacked boxes sure of what I am trying to find when a group of laborers start shouting me what am I doing here and chasing me in and around all the various rows and pilings I hide in an open box until eventually cornered by a group of men threating to close the box and leave me in it an Asian man appears who seems to be in charge begins to argue with one of the men takes out some kind of pitchfork and lunges with it at the man's neck decapitates him the head rolling onto the ground then more men appear and more fighting allows me enough time to escape move oversize bags of planter box soil from the front of the house to the rear one by one throwing them up on my shoulder cautiously walking round back where I drop them Molly fills the planters with soil plants pepper tomato and cucumber plants in the thin strip of land that borders our property and our neighbor the sunniest spot on our land roast a whole chicken with mushrooms pappardelle with a tomato and cucumber salad watch movie with aging Tom Berringer who shoots and kills a bank robber with a bag full of loot in a hunting accident in the Maine wilderness drive to Gloucester with Michele share our stories of the Italian-American immigrant experience fathers and mothers the good and bad the food the treatment of women the anger rage trauma violence of working class experience walk around Stage Fort Park put our feet in the icy Atlantic at Half Moon Beach visit John at the house fried clams at a local joint on the pier long drive back to rural Taunton suburb where her family lives talk books life teaching love music she'll head back to North Carolina on Thursday painters arrive early in the morning to begin touch up work on the outside of the house read opening to student short stories writer I don't know harassing me on Facebook for information about my publishers writes as writers we must do everything we can to get the attention of publishers he's got cred he says sends me reviews of his books such a shame our tribe so desperate and shameless to get their work out I wonder when humans first began to paint on cave walls were they desperate for an audience or a gallery to show their work millions of books where do they go I think of the thousands of books on my shelves most will be tossed when I am gone why write at all I ask myself time and again I don't have an answer something inside drives me to it I need it like water why are we the only animals that want our expression and signals to stick around meet Dave for espresso at the Italian café outside tables full old-timers tease talk loudly shout at heightened pitches we can hardly hear ourselves talk family music writing pandemic recovery two guys at corner table count hundred dollar bills into packs of ten place them in leather bag must be at least twenty thousand walk along Mystic River ducks geese snow geese cormorants herons Orange Line trains crisscrossing same bridge my mother and I would over a half century ago on our way in and out of the North End for food shopping past Assembly Square Winter Hill Yacht Club Amelia Earhart Dam old man fishing strike up conversation talk about the old days Somerville Medford fishing gentrification he rolls his own cigarettes offers me one thank him no been a lot of years at his age he says no reason to think about stopping families lovers teenagers out walking en masse and maskless easy to feel the pandemic never really happened but still a threat health officials warn breezy humid morning sit out on the patio sun and moon opposite sides of sky take in Molly's plants and flowers boy next door playing with his father already coming up on two years old write it where does the time go mystery is an essential element in creativity when a bird calls the clouds become more mysterious pay less attention to words it is written look more to the spaces between them this is called the importance of the spaces between words feel free to make mistakes if you do just continue this is known as don't let mistakes get in your way what is vs. the idea of what is eliminate the blocks you can't escape

Julia and Celeste home for Father's Day ravioli with marinara sauce sauteed spinach with garlic and olive oil chocolate cake with butter cream frosting morning tea on the patio Molly's flowers burst everywhere bird song drowned out by air conditioners shouts of construction workers their trucks pull in and out unloading tools and stock six houses within sight of ours under construction what we know what is known only figures of speech we each make meaning of the day yet only sight and experience mean the sky is filled with crystal forms raise your glass up in a toast entrust your body to the elements switch over to poetry from fiction in summer writing class Jim sends photos from Rafe's Chasm stripers he caught fishing today writes he's trying to find a balance between walking swimming fishing and household duties she writes that she will not be going to China after all Yuan Hung-tao writes that sooner or later our words will be eaten away by moss or effaced by wind and rain but for now they are cut in stone sixty-five years old what have I accomplished I'm like a boat struggling upstream gains a foot loses two who says there are flowers that never fade the universe is blown by wind into an ocean of clouds I can't bare to face the day right now how many poems books theories read how many asanas how many steps how many ways to look at the nature of this existence some mornings it feels impossible to swing my feet out from the bed who was it that said you've got to fight for survival long Revere Beach walk quiet today scattered groups of teenagers and twenty-somethings on the sand old-timers strewn along the boardwalk small groups or alone dark over-tanned leathery skin talk days that have been smoke cigarettes and cigars occasional joggers and cyclists gulls swoop from air pockets or hunker down in small groups on the shore suddenly police cars speed past sirens blare flashing lights all stop far down the beach wonder will they be there when I reach then disperse several onto the sand rush up and down the shoreline others back out on the boulevard stop for water sit on the wall waves forceful in high tide peak sun hot on my face and arms memorial party for Margo large crowd many friends I haven't seen since the pandemic anecdotes poems music memories from family and a lifetime of friends lots of booze and food mood shifts with alcohol consumption and I never knew that Margo once dated Lennie Tristano but I did know she liked Italian men I'm working in a restaurant and get into an argument with a customer who claims I ordered food from another restaurant and put it on his bill and if I don't remove the charge off of his bill he will call the police on me I'm running around trying to find my manager but she is nowhere in sight the restaurant is so overcrowded it is some kind of graduation day and we are overbooked you don't have to live in the wild to be a recluse perhaps Nature is perfect but human society is full of ups and downs where do we find real happiness for years I've studied and practiced the Tao but gotten nowhere my mind remains a tangled knot Brickbottom where spacious condo lofts house local artists and once I insulted a painter about her work hanging in a show there where once tenement rows and slaughterhouses one of the earliest sections of the city to gentrify and since then city unrecognizable over the last thirty years meet Mitch for coffee talk Buddha Tao Yuan Mei Yuan Hung-tao Malcolm X Nerval Olson H.D. labor studies anarchism how to exorcise the machinery of the productivity culture from our lives the do more be more achieve more who needs drive-thru poetry Mitch's trip to Chicago next week with Gabe Mitch's notebooks swell with poems he reads Kenneth Patchen to me at a sidewalk table at the café how to keep oneself clean from a society of people who want to be seen Celeste and Julia packing up Celeste's belongings moving her to her very first apartment loading the cars unloading them to return and start all over again July 4th weekend cold temps heavy rain two carloads of men on Route 95 wearing camouflage wielding long guns and pistols refuse to surrender to the state police they do not acknowledge authority of the government new track and field star stripped of her awards and medals cannot go to the Olympics baseball star suspended for a week for assaulting a woman who gets to make the laws what purpose they serve who decides where what and when they are prescribed news on this Independence Day the date that Henry David Thoreau moved to Walden Pond that people no longer allowed to swim on open water in the pond don't know what TikTok is have no interest in ever knowing Zoom meeting with Michele and Dan Michele grieving over her mother's eminent death they'll be in Boston next month let's spend another day together for the first time since we brought Julia home nearly twenty-five years ago it's only Molly and me the girls' room empty both working and living on their own promise to come home and visit more rain more clouds day after day tomato pepper cucumber and herb plants coming in slow read the last of summer course short stories feel like it's been a never-ending strain since March 2020 when the lockdown came and we switched over to online classes have stopped looking at the news Trump still the best-selling story in the country cops still shooting people racism and sexism still rule poor getting poorer rich richer it's the same old story all of the glory is a pantomime thousands of universes have been blown by wind into oceans of clouds yet humans remain toxic unwilling see beyond this world look at Shaq's newest yacht NFL star Rob Gronkowski loves these shoes Carson reveals details of Gen and Blake's vows sixty-five game-changing zucchini recipes Kim Kardashian falls into water while water boarding Kourtney Kardashian strips down to a lacy bra co-hosts of the *The View* were reportedly at their wit's end TikToks simple blackhead removal that actually works Paulina Porizkova fifty-six shares stripped-down mirror selfie Quentin Tarantino says Burt Reynolds died happy Gwyneth Paltrow eating carbs and drinking wine I spend $300 a week on my wellness routine Demi Moore and daughter look like twins happy puppy born without eyes Rebel Wilson goes boating in low-cut turquoise swimsuit after many days of heavy rain and dark clouds sun breaks through clouds water in the basement Molly's garden sodden my right hip joint aches from the weeklong damp slow yoga session drive to Gloucester for Willie and Anne's art opening Anne's gripping photographs of Gloucester's essence the beat buildings houses fences and alleys Willie's brilliant abstracts painted during the pandemic talk with Amanda Jim Willie Annie Henry Gregor Brian and lots of other friends I haven't seen in a while walk Half Moon Beach under starlight water calm party boat out on the harbor loud dance music boatload of partiers singing in unison blasting across the harbor in all directions stop in to visit John at the house steak tips at a pub frequented by locals then long quiet drive back to the city Yuan Hung-tao observed that ants have eyes so it's curious they depend on antennae for forward movement so he recorded the matter for future scholars of living creatures Mitch writes he and Gabe have left Chicago and headed for the Motor City I'm in the mood for a roast chicken so will head for the market soon Oxford St. blocked Central St. blocked detour up to Highland Ave. heavy morning traffic all the way onto Expressway backed up beyond Somerville state police cruisers posted at intervals along the way pulling cars over in express lane that only have one person in vehicle traffic down to a crawl so people can watch as they drive by down into the tunnel Coltrane rips it up on "Blues Minor" signal fades in the tunnel out onto the Mass. Pike west eastern traffic bumper to bumper all the way out to Route 95 for the morning commute translate with her all day on one long passage a monster on the horizon Phoenix melting in the sky not sure if readers will understand what you are doing I don't care she replies she tells me as a young girl before she heard or read stories she listened to the stories that the mountains and rivers told her and people didn't understand that it is said the world's filled with power spirits deities wind rain rocks animals plants people all have power in them change is part of it all and to understand change is to understand the movement of the Tao in all things all things originate in the Tao and return to the Tao this is known as all things emerge and return to the Tao drive to Malden Square outdoor live music show featuring Fireking park the car no outdoor show to be seen stop in at Cultural Center to inquire that's next Saturday not this Saturday drive to café for an espresso too crowded to get in head back home take a long nap instead wake to more rain the most rainy July on record cook dinner baked chicken thighs with mushrooms fresh herbs and white wine broccoli sauteed in garlic olive oil and a squeeze of lemon rain heavy throughout the night thunder blasts and lightning into the morning tea on front porch Julia cancels breakfast plans missed her train home from her friend's last night go out for breakfast anyway eggs toast home fries coffee start work on syllabi for fall classes two of three never taught before must start from scratch guy next door playing the electric guitar in his garage lower back still sore nearly a week unable to get around well or do yoga mending slowly but causing great discomfort who moves the sun moon and stars in their due motion towards their stations this is known as the question of who moves the sun moon and stars towards their stations it is said there was a time when people were able to go up into the sky and come down again this was known as going up to the sky and coming down again in the 1780s Ten Hills Farm stretched all around the Mystic River Basin up through Medford Governor Winthrop a street and a town named after him owned slaves many of whom were Native Americans lunch with Amanda talk love Gerrit family friendships Gloucester why write poetry at all and the plague of the po-biz and the significance of her long Olson poem pull out rug in my studio ruined by water damage throw it out in the trash air out the studio burn incense pain in lower back continues still unable to do yoga somewhere there is someone whose ear ornaments are two green snakes and rides two dragons his name is Lord of the Summer who flew high into the sky and brought songs down to earth and became the first person to sing things like this make me hopeful for the future long after I am gone and my dust mingled with void begin work on annual faculty report gather syllabi write file for each course taught procedures texts read assignments go over every teaching detail from September 2020 to May 2021 then fill out university form listing duties courses taught department service advising mentoring letters of recommendation reading committees break in the rain dry sunny day first mushroom walk of the season in state forest woods wet mosquitoes swarm hike around Julia's Loop how many times now in the past fifteen years through the pines down through the wetlands up and over the granite knoll down through the old pine stand into the hardwoods cool damp woodsy air clear sky birds abundant singing songs about the Tao mushrooms aplenty most old waterlogged bug-eaten pick a modest amount of boletes saute with butter eat them in a crusty sandwich with asiago cheese another drizzly morning rain in the forecast next six days sit on front porch with tea wind coaxing the swaying trees jets drum high above the clouds chance meeting in café old high school friend Lucille looks the same as she did as a teenager she has a son with her who has Down Syndrome named Ben worked as an engineer now retired then she's not Lucille and tells me she left some pot buried in the hill behind the high school and it's probably still there we could drive there and dig it up but my car is missing from the parking lot weed-wack the driveway take clippers to the stubborn ones sweep into a pile before heavy rains sky darkens near black thunder lightning and severe downpour day after day rain clouds thunderstorms marinade chicken in lemon and fresh basil then broil cucumber and golden pepper salad edit excerpt from her novel to submit for publication how's the summer vacation you ask just finished teaching a summer course now prepping for fall classes and working on faculty report the activity of teaching never ceases facemasks mandated on campus until October virus on the rise again and a variant people still refuse vaccine Jim writes he bought two Johnny Thunders albums for six bucks each at a used record store when stars pour down they proclaim their occupation of the world then midnight swallows everything man's body pulled from the Charles River near the B.U. Bridge witnesses saw him struggling to stay afloat before he disappeared under the murky water more work cleaning and organizing my studio no more room for books shelves full and spilling over books piled high on surfaces who will read them when I am gone for twenty-seven years the eighty-one-year-old man's lived in a solar-powered wood plank cabin on the shore of the Merrimack River grows his own vegetables raises chickens drinks spring-fed water greets boaters on the river refuses to leave the seventy-three-acre privately owned woodlot so they've put him in jail which he prefers to being turned over to social services oh Henry oh David Olson said you were not thorough enough giant oak tree between two three-deckers leveled and shredded in four hours old woman pink hat white dress cardboard box I don't know names of birds that call continually in the early morning but each voice is distinct nothing like the other who claims that humans inhabit this neighborhood the morning sky is full of the Great Clod's forms and I feel the dustiness of my meager life there are those who can journey underground others fly to the stars still others travel to the bottom of the deepest seas yet most never leave the chair they sit in despite travel to the corners of the world this is known as traveling far and wide yet going nowhere first time riding the subway since the pandemic Julia and I train to Boston walk streets of the North End I show her memory spots from my childhood buildings my relatives and grandparents lived in alleys in which my cousins and I played games Copps Hill Cemetery where my cousin Vinny hid his nudie books under a fallen gravestone Snow Hill Street where we wheeled speedily down in carts made from salvaging fruit and vegetable crates at Haymarket and attaching roller skate wheels and the Parado with the statue of Paul Revere where my grandfather took me and I splashed in the fountain water while he hung out with old Italian friends smoking and talking in a language I did not understand and the North End Pool where my grandmother took us having packed crusty meatball sandwiches and fruit and we swam and played until the end of the day and the restaurant where my godfather Rocco once had a pastry shop and the restaurant that was Tony the Butcher where my mother bought her meat espresso at Café Vittoria then down to Chinatown lunch at Gourmet Dumpling House dumplings tofu fish with ginger and scallion Chinese greens over the Chinese bakery where Julia buys Chinese buns with sausages inside sit in the park watching tourists and old Chinese people play mahjong and the old Chinese man wants to sell a jade bracelet for three hundred dollars no thanks so he offers a jade necklace for twenty talk of life past present future back to subway Julia finds a cell phone dials a contact connects with a voice the owner's mother did you lose a cell phone yes well I have it where are you State Street ok stay there we are on the way c'mon dad we're going to State Street and she returns the person's phone Orange Line back to Somerville drop Julia off great to see you great to see you quick as a breeze lifts a child grows up and my flesh continues to sag and hair continues to gray one note sung by a bird below the setting sun John writes we're on for the trip to Gloucester next weekend my first stay in the cabin since before Gerrit died fresh pesto tossed with rigatoni and chopped cherry tomatoes everything from Molly's garden flavors explode in the mouth tea on the porch sun rise over the trees these moments swallow me up life after life come and go the same sun and moon rise and set meet Frankie for lunch Frankie oldest and best friend from childhood first time we see each other since the pandemic talk marriage divorce music our youth addiction old age what to do in our remaining years our children his grandson his business my teaching mistakes we've made what we're grateful for death waiting for us not too far away politics the state of the country compared with what we expected fifty years ago when we believed things would change for the better tripping on acid in Medford Square where we'd spy his father passed out drunk on a bench beatings at the hand of my father and let's not wait so long until our next meeting autumn in the air this morning cool and rainy drop my car off at garage for repairs wet walk home more work on faculty report breakfast of Celeste's banana bread with fruit and tea email from Peter who has tickets for us to see Steve Forbett on August 20 let's meet early and have dinner beforehand he's playing his piano again first time in twenty years one more revision on his novel then he will send the draft for me to read I am grateful to be alive to be clean and sober to have real friends and two amazing daughters who love me despite all my mistakes this moment in time gray day lush greens flitting in breeze rain striking roof and vinyl siding of house all this will never be the same Molly and I are raising chickens in the yard they are beginning to lay eggs of all different sizes and colors but when I try to collect them the chickens swarm around to prevent me I am only able to grab one at a time I drop several as I try to run into the house the eggs look like colored pancakes in the frying pan but taste like eggs when I eat them the chickens are not really chickens and they disappear underground and we can't find them midsummer has just ended yet the morning air has a chill Molly's vegetables slow to ripen cold spring too much summer rain not enough sun so much of the poetry I read today bores me bring me the poems of friends that always bring a thrill or old masters from some far away place who still live through their words being old is good for getting up early to sit and meditate on everyone who has gone before me grateful to be alive this day to steep my tea sit on the front porch amongst the flowers trees birds and listen to the day take shape people walk to the bus stop workmen pull up in their trucks traffic slowly increases with the whir of tires the sky brightens and I'm not sure the importance of the plan I have in mind Julia drops by to do laundry the washer in her apartment broke saw a man and a woman fucking in a pickup truck in a parking lot this afternoon in Revere the woman on top facing the windshield the man's feet on the dashboard his toes opening and closing with his thrusts at any given time a number of events can occur depending on what has happened before we are not locked into a predetermined destiny if we understand the nature of change we can alter the possibilities of our own actions this is known as altering the possibilities of our own actions if we

prepare for death while we live we can leave life in
the proper way this is known as getting ready to die
beside littered railroad tracks overgrown weeds and
toppled shopping carts junk tires trash graffiti red-
brick backside of old Derby Desk factory building
rehabbed multi-level neighbor's house now three
condos selling for over one million each peach tree
in my other neighbor's yard full of ripe and rotting
peaches that litter the ground spend the day in
Gloucester with Michele and Dan visiting from
South Carolina swim at Half Moon Beach North
Atlantic Ocean warm and buoyant walk along the
coast music jam on John's front porch Dan on tenor
guitar Michele on uke me on six-string acoustic
sharing vocals swapping songs John and Cecilia
arrive join in on vocals pan-seared haddock dinner
by the ocean brilliant quarter moon follows us on
our drive back into the city when younger I had
many strong cravings now that I am old they've
gradually slipped away I've bought so many books
they spill over everywhere most I will never read
again I return to the same ones over and over my
daughters now grown never read books it's hard to
get students to read books all the pages in my library
fade slowly decay as do bindings until pages begin
to fall out yet I still can't let them go my markings
and margin notes no longer clear or meaningful my
life has been full of meetings and partings sadness

and joy my right hip aches down to the knee sneaking up for years from occasional light soreness to a constant discomfort and sometimes pain this is known as old age for which there is no reward come whisper to me in my sleepless night-hours touch my hand soon the sun will rise then warp into the day of tasks and meaning only to disappear into empty yesterday until the leaves begin to dry up change color blown away into the winter of our death this is known as leaves fall and blow away I've decided to shave my head need an electric razor my mother says she will help me pick one out we go to Harvard Square an old men's shop and she questions the salesman about them I used to be a hairdresser she tells him when he seems amused that she knows so much about electric razors we get separated in the square and I rush down various streets looking for her nowhere to be found I stop at a café for an espresso and sit outside hoping she'll pass several of my students walk by say hello stop to talk about upcoming semester and having to wear masks and be vaccinated I offer to buy them an ice cream and they sit down but they are not my students they are visiting from out of state and ask me if I am a monk I am wearing an orange robe and my head is shaved and I tell them I am living in a nearby monastery moved in several months ago training to be a monk and explain about the Way and deciding to dedicate my life Celeste texts and says she and Reed found a good place for donuts the nightmare can stay put the plan on hold to be honest I'm scared the stitching of a well-made blouse fly in sequence together under your breath I remember falling on my head I remember wishing my father was dead I remember my first cigarette with Patty behind the Curtis School I remember my mother singing in the kitchen I remember my father dancing the cha-cha I remember when Gina Tambini broke my heart I remember learning how to swim at Wright's Pond I remember kicking a dog I remember delicious soup I remember when I first discovered Jackson Pollock I remember my first guitar I remember loneliness in the backyard I remember my beagle Spotty I remember the deluge of snow in '68/'69 I remember crying when President Kennedy was shot I remember my mother's home made ravioli I remember my first trip to New York City I remember spin the bottle I remember learning to drive I remember my first acid trip I remember my manual typewriter I remember teaching my first class I remember pumping gas I remember playing baseball in the little league I remember geese flying south I remember when I believed in Santa I remember looking out my grandparents' North End apartment on Christmas Eve looking for him in the sky I remember when I believed in God I remember my first girlfriend Helen Centofanti I remember when the city flooded Hickey Park and we played hockey in winter that curtain you hold back allowing a certain slant of light to fall upon the wood floor is fact not myth who is the poem for in times of reconciliation of self they're tearing down the building that stood for separate individuals in order to make room for little feet to meet and share cookies if there's milk then drink but mostly birds bomb still waters where water creatures become extinct think mermaids think tentacles think falling to dark depths hold your breath hurricane warnings for southern Massachusetts and Cape Cod heavy rain brings more water into the basement concerns about returning to campus this fall overcrowded shuttle busses overcrowded classrooms improper ventilation in buildings delta variant spreading across the country must prepare to switch over to remote in the event of another campus shutdown the past weighs me down I don't remember who I am did my hand every really touch yours I cannot escape shame whose light never stops shining on me oh to return home sleep soundly in my own bed out to see first live music show since before the pandemic masks required indoors except when taking a sip from your drink doesn't feel the same masked trying to dance gasping for air though the beat still digs deep and moves from the inside out Hurricane

Henri never hit much fuss about it for several days leads to nothing it is written that the Sky God looks like an ox has eight feet two heads and a horse's tail drones like a beetle and wherever he appears you can expect war in books you meet the people of old whose bones have turned to dust on the street you meet the people of today it is good that one need not belong to their own time this is known as not belonging to one's own time we all have a spark of the Tao inside but craving and mindless thought prevent that spark from developing dominated by analytical thinking and internal chatter the Great Clod burdens us with forms rise at 4 A.M. drive Celeste to the airport wrong turn on the way back end up on the Mass. Pike west get off at exit wind my way through Cambridge and Somerville to home roads rivers sidewalks highways are pathways along which energy flows the natural world is the model of uncorrupted reality there is little mercy in that world all things hang on survival society demands social conventions like poetic form best avoid the authorities follow the path that swells up in the individual mind and heart and knows no rules and regulations Amanda writes just to say I have read the books you sent me and which you were probably writing for years forgive me they were delicious so salty so cool Celeste texts that she arrived in El Paso I text send photos of the meals you eat bread chicken thighs bake serve with basil couscous and sauteed broccoli with garlic and olive oil cell phone won't charge go to Apple Store at Cambridge Galleria Mall technician cleans the charging port there you go all set now wow I thought I'd have to buy a new cell phone for two months now I've been sitting meditation returning to an old form of years ago right leg very tender unable to sit lotus stretch leg out straight the mind still willing to slow down around this time of year I begin to think about hen-of-the-woods mushrooms all the rain could bring a bountiful crop in October I have a feeling that old age has come for good can the simplest person and the most learned be measured by the same rules what suits a fish does not please a bird once there was a man with a broom who tried to sweep the clouds away he swept and swept to his death and the clouds never ceased swirling and morphing this is known as don't try to sweep the clouds away Jim writes he's back from PA dropped Seamus off at Penn State return drive through Hurricane Henri strong winds heavy rains and how he caught more fish during the pandemic because he felt more a part of the ecosystem not apart from it he became one with the rocks sea seagulls cormorants the sky aligned with the sea rewarded him humbly with a fish here and there how he thanked the stars kissed the fish and put them back from whence they came like people days and nights are never the same chilly today hot tomorrow humid tonight tomorrow night not rain hard one day sunny sky the next heavy fog one night bright stars another last night clouds began to shroud the moon soon it was nowhere to be seen wind picked up a tree fell down on the street one day the night settled into stillness hail has been known to fall hard day or night some days begin sunny and turn gray some nights start out cold and by morning temps have risen some days leaves appear other days fall away the moon changes every night on a recent night a dog barked for hours wet heavy snow falls some days a light dusting sometimes it snows all night and day today sunny and humid we remember yesterday and the night before too much time passes all days all nights blur into bottleneck of memory while change and impermanence never cease Jim writes he spent the day fishing on a houseboat in Plum Island caught a bluefish and a big striper tomorrow morning he drops Gavin off at UMass Lowell Julia and Celeste bring BBQ and cake for my birthday talk about Celeste's business trip to El Paso and Julia's road trip around mid-America and all the states where she would never live now she writes that Xin Xin has returned from China and will begin school next week and let's translate on Tuesday I still don't know if Haiyang fucked the woman in the neighborhood who hangs out at the bridge and teases all the men or if Su Hui only imagines that he did the reader doesn't have to know she says Dr. Onkamon texts to confirm my oral surgery on Thursday three hours under the knife three or four days to recover liquid and soft food only I buy ice cream and milk and will live on milkshakes email from the English department would I be interested in teaching a fourth course next semester 6 American Authors one of my favorite courses to teach yes I would be interested in teaching four courses this 25% increase in pay for half a year the old Japanese woman in her apartment who puts fresh flowers on table at building's main entrance stands on her balcony overlooking the parking lot holding objects in her hand when someone pulls in the lot she drops it asks the person to pick it up bring it to her apartment heavy rain left over from Hurricane Ida lots of water in the basement 4:30 A.M. sweeping water into the drain floods down south floods in New York City rivers flowing down subway stairs wettest summer I can ever recall email from UMass beginning of semester checklist Julia drops by picks up stuff she left by accident the other night her plan to take a trip to Burlington Vermont Indigenous Peoples weekend it is said everyone is already a Buddhist and has a Buddhist heart but that heart must be awakened and cultivated Mitch enters the café reads from the poem he wrote on the way the subtracted life is out I'm in for expansion and discovery of seeing and action in the unified being talk the corporatization of the poem and education spirit teaching how to live in this world avoid the toxic ether that surrounds us in the media on campus in advertising in it's this or that the latest trends how to make amends how to lose unwanted fat to get back what's been stolen and held from us usurped thoughts and feelings and out on Main Street traffic's backed up drivers lean on horns across the street Medford Bodhisattva walks oversized in short sleeve shirt shorts black socks sneakers blue umbrella awhirl over his shoulder Mitch says that's why we came here today to see him pass we are time beings in time being phenomena of the primordial mirror of mind three hours in the dentist chair for oral surgery cut open gum drill two holes into the gum to install implants but they won't fit more drilling and tapping finally implants snug the raw mess sutured over unable to eat drink milkshakes for two days then slowly soft foods then regular food but only to be chewed on the opposite side of the new implants it is said one cannot become enlightened by a set method of teachings but by an internally intuitive process which is spontaneous and part of one's own inner nature this is known as following one's own inner nature Charlie Watts drummer for Rolling Stones dead media full of stories and memories each time a baby boomer rock star or sports hero dies the baby boomers turn on the nostalgia tears return to feelings attached to sights and sounds from long ago losing another piece of their pasts that once had importance long long ago unable to grasp the insignificance of everything they hold dear trapped in the unrealistic significance of a song or a home run in the no time being 5 A.M. Jim writes from Rafe's Chasm about Cassandra who threw herself into the sea last November how sometimes he can hear the seer siren song of the ocean on the rocks she swims and sleeps in these moments how a seal surfaced did a side stroke looked at him dove back into eternity Dear Mei Yao Chen the children have grown I am old you said it would come to this someone hammers in the oncoming evening there is no silence even if I whisper the poem turns on itself a moraine under the patterns of stars in the onset of night within the curl of the brush hush in the horse's hooves you look for white jade but within a steady gaze colors blur be careful not to nourish a bird with what would nourish you define loneliness beneath a sigh left behind these masses that settle into plastic trees green skyward flash aspects of things beyond formation where misleadingly unknown to us they lead territories like edges partition themselves then disappear nothing is permanent you you you and you the young pregnant woman pushes her toddler in a carriage I manage my whole afternoon wrapped in her world nothing seems more real than this woman her toddler and the carriage wheels rolling along a sidewalk stops at a crosswalk to wait for the signal to cross whatever this world means to say is spoken all of it in this moment just because something is known by a name it does not mean it is known by that name only that it is known by that name and just because a person is known by a name it does not mean that is their name only that they are known by that name this is known as not being known by what you are known by arbitrary conceptions of things and people a sonnet is not really a sonnet but an illusion of a sonnet the Great Clod burdens us with forms it is said Nature generates heart heart generates mind mind generates emotion emotion generates illusion this the human way of being return to emotion by filtering illusion return emotion to mind gather the mind to stabilize the heart return the heart to the place of Nature on my way to a party in Cambridge gathering of poets local and out of town up from Harvard Square T-stop across the Yard through Museum of Natural History crowded apartment smell of pot smoke beer and wine loud conversations fill each room largest group in the kitchen gather around Iggy Pop talking about haiku talk with Levi introduces me to his female friend but she wants to meet Iggy everything too claustrophobic for me so I leave without say goodbye to anyone back through Museum of Natural History across the Yard to T-stop but I don't have my phone I must have left it at the party so many things we have to keep track of now weren't part of our lives years ago back across the Yard Museum of Natural History isn't where it should be I go searching for it asking people on the street which street is the Museum of Natural History lost wandering in the square rise very early in the dark make my bed brew tea sit on front porch in pre-dawn silence morning star in fading night sky hangs above long feather of cloud sun breaks through clouds lights up Bunker Hill Memorial traffic light on expressway to UMass parking lot shuttle bus to campus students packed into classrooms check in with colleagues most of whom I haven't seen since March 2020 my office cluttered and messy the way I left it the night I was teaching a class and a text arrived everyone leave the campus at once the campus and classrooms are overcrowded run around campus doing beginning-of-semester tasks fire drills in two main buildings separate times classrooms empty out big rush down stairs to exit doors only to be let back in again exhausted by end of day shuttle bus to parking lot and car slow crawl from parking lot to logjammed Expressway snake my way to Somerville exit and home big dinner to fill my hunger go to bed early sleep for nine hours rise this morning yoga meditation tea on porch life is a gathering of energy body and mind unified body is the foundation of the mind mind is the essence of the body first week down at school campus overcrowded too much construction students detoured jams at exits and entrances difficult to hear the students behind masks when they talk in class but students earnest working hard making the best of a scary situation legs ache end of day after standing four hours during class time and walking around campus and up and down stairs roads heavy traffic to Expressway late in the afternoon cars backed up all the way to the Somerville exit neighbor's apple tree weighed down with apples ripe and rotten falling ground laden with them mornings grow cooler but each day reaches high temps and humidity still lingering no one is locked into a destiny they cannot change though some believe it so once there was a man crossed a busy highway for seventy-seven straight days and on the seventy-eighth he got struck by a car and died this is known and knowing when to stop I try to measure my relationship with the Earth what is this force beneath my feet it is said some stars have negative effects and some have positive effects be careful which stars you befriend my friend Gerrit the avatar chose to mingle amongst humans taking the appearance of a mortal to inspire instruct and advise Pao-kuang star tip of the Big Dipper's handle cycling around the center clear cool night conservation area walk late afternoon downhill through hardwoods and pines squirrels and chipmunks abound on ground up and down trees out into large expanse of field hawk circumnavigates the air pockets above woman walking with leash did I see a brown lab no if I do give a shout path winds through the tall grass late season insects working the wildflowers circling around into more woods small pond glass still except for occasional fish bubbles mother with two children mom can I catch a frog no leave the frogs alone what have they ever done to you but I won't hurt it I promise continue on out into the field climb up hill back into the woods woman with her brown lab on leash found him sun falling behind the tree line woods darkening birdsong flows on air can't find the short path out to parking lot back down realize I turned the wrong way at the fork in the path back up and out to the car stop at Bella Ravioli pick up homemade cheese ravioli back home pick a bowl of fresh tomatoes and fresh basil cut tomatoes quick run through blender saute chopped garlic and crushed red pepper add tomatoes and salt cook high for ten minutes add chopped basil slab of butter and serve over boiled ravioli with grated cheese rise at six tea on porch yoga then meditation read student childhood memories from creative writing class coming to America from Puerto Rico attempted rape by her brother being left at the kiddie park having four siblings he never knew he had fascination with Tinker Bell a grandfather who read her stories and gave her the gift of storytelling first day of school in a new town watching 9/11 on the television too young to understand what's happening friend writes he's reading my memoir could I help him stop drinking I'll help in any way I can Michele writes do I want to do a show with her and Dan at a pub in Taunton Gian writes he was sick most of the summer with Lyme anemia will be weeks before he's feeling better student writes will I be grading papers because he submitted one and hasn't got a grade I write yes but I have one hundred students please allow a week or so for me to respond to your assignments Mitch writes he's working his ass off this semester can't seem to get caught up seems all he's doing is prepping and reading assignments Lucy writes about her childhood in China how she stole food vouchers from her parents to buy candy and when they found out her father beat the palms of her hands with a stick Celeste Reed and his brother Will drop by the Italian café where I am having an espresso at a table out front finish first batch of reading from my creative writing class tomorrow short reflections are due from three more classes they've closed down

Highland Ave. for some kind of festival drive across the city around to Somerville Ave. up the hill down a one-way street to get to Oxford Street and home waiting for a spell of cool nights to bring out the hen-of-the-woods mushrooms which should be plentiful with all the rain this summer this morning coolest of the season blanket wrap sip tea on front porch workmen across the street switch to sweatshirts and long pants boughs on neighbor's apple tree droop apples litter the ground wild geese call from some distant corner of sky the activity of the world never ceases breathe the essence of the Cosmos deep in and out lose the conversation in my head let the particles ascend to the distant reaches of the void three classes' worth of short reflections dropped into Blackboard sip tea read and respond to the first round air cooling down leaves beginning to show traces of color shifts my old cravings slip away with age won't be long I will travel to some place beyond here where my eyes will see things they have never seen seems a day a month a year or ten are nothing I am quite certain once I had some plan in mind I saw myself going in a certain direction yet all those things that mattered in life are so easy to break with soon I will be too old to write poetry best not to repeat oneself like the Tao the poem that can be named is not the real poem time is free like Nature the time that can be told is not the real time what is is not all there is the construction worker on campus says fuckin' in every sentence we gotta get this fuckin' thing squared away this isn't in fuckin' line somebody measure how many fuckin' feet between these two fuckin' lines somebody get my fuckin' hammer give me a fuckin' cigarette I gotta tell you I'm glad it's fuckin' Friday this has been a long fuckin' week and I'm glad to see it come to a fuckin' end you know what I'm fuckin' talkin' about Dear Professor I have to write a letter I am applying for an internship in a publishing company could you help me write it Dear Yuong yes I can try to help write a first draft then send it to me I'll read it then we can have a meeting Dear Professor I'm sorry I will not be in class today I have a sore throat and nasal congestion Dear Professor I know you said we didn't have to send you that piece we brought in for class discussion I wonder should I send it in anyway sitting around John's kitchen table in Gloucester talk about Kerouac Diane di Prima Olson and what is projective Jim and Gabe read their poems Gabe and Jim swim at Half Moon Beach way out beyond the rocks we tease John after all these years he is finally beginning to like poetry plan a mushroom walk for October I give Jim the painting of Wieners that Derek gave to me years ago time for Jim to bring John home where he belongs wandering down Highland Ave. he forgets names and locations of streets he knows he knows and I too someday will lose my way unable to stay inside the lines marked out who will come to the rescue secure me on the path where the dark man turns to wave me on c'mon c'mon won't be long I can see it in his eyes move along move along your song nears its end best not to think any corner of the world is far away all one has to do is open a page and you will get there this is known books can take you to any corner of the world one's real age is the age of the books one is reading the older I grow the more I try to cherish every minute yet still can't rid myself of getting annoyed worried or anxious I used to drink to bring me pleasure that became a dead end now I must refrain process pleasure and pain without false filters the Tao contains thunder lightning sunshine and moonlight but all phenomena known to man cannot fill up the Tao and we can never know what the Tao has in mind no mind is its mind this is known as the Tao has no mind yet contains all minds I must train my way of being in the world a clear path will only get in the way slip into patterns that are out there without naming them this is known as slipping into patterns and not naming them which is another way of saying lose your mind loosen the world before it loses you wake at 2 A.M. unable to fall back to sleep rise at 4:15 tea on the porch sit meditation breakfast cod liver oil banana and two eggs shower out the door early park car in lot ignore shuttle bus walk to campus salt air of the bay sun and wispy clouds seagulls call from wind pockets jets depart and arrive at Logan people travel and return from faraway every day neat little cars on congested highways show me the way show me the way show me the way to go home I'll stretch yawn and sit right back in my comfy chair where there they're or their are only words everyone's busy on the new job the person that hired me is taking me around introducing me folks friendly everyone knows each other seems like the kind of place where it's all one big team and all the players happy to be there not sure what kind of business it is I get taken from one meeting to another coffee and pastries and lots of joking around amongst the people follow this one follow that one department to another but I see no products or jobs being done though everyone looks to be busy and talking about where they are at in this project or that and where they will go next though there's nothing for me to do at the end of a week I'm getting familiar with people who seem to accept me but all I do is walk around nothing to do then I see him in his plaid jacket looking just like I see him in the media and realized it is a Donald Trump reality show I am taken aback everyone is circling around him vying for his attention he's standing over someone on a table performing acupuncture on them I'm next somebody says but I don't want to be in fact I hate Donald Trump and I don't even know how I ended up here Julia and I walk for mushrooms on Julia's Loop in the state forest trail overgrown from all the summer rain mushrooms everywhere though we decide to focus mostly on hen-of-the-woods Julia spots a fresh batch of black trumpets we decide to harvest then continue along the trail ascend the granite knoll as the trail winds towards the top the high point and half way mark of our loop when Julia shouts out Dad I turn she's pointing to a beautiful specimen of hen-of-the-woods says you walked right past it we hug to celebrate harvest the mushroom carefully reach the top of the knoll stop for a rest and water Julia cleans and dresses the scrape on my hand from when I slipped on the rocks pulls out Dunkin' Donuts butterscotch donuts I eat my first donut in years we catch our breaths retell the story of finding the hen-of-the-woods and how I walked right by it before we descend the knoll back down to the main part of the trail and walk back to the car in the parking lot Jim writes from Rafe's Chasm about standing at the face of the vast distance of unknowable sea cast and reel in over and over until a lightning strike battle with a fighting creature of the sea until you pull it up on the rocks the closest thing to meditation or religion he has right now and throwing the fish back into the ocean the most sacred thing he does all day fish is his hen-of-the-woods even washing dishes is sacred depending on how you move through the universe most of the media and politician vaccine deniers have been vaccinated continue to urge others to their deaths for ad money and votes first student of the semester in one of my classes to test positive I have to wait three to five days then get tested Monday morning at nine test results back in one day negative how many more students will test positive how many more tests will I have to take baked chicken thighs with sage white wine and hen-of-the-woods mushrooms couscous and broccoli sauteed with garlic and olive oil energy inside the body is connected to energy of the Cosmos it is this energy that brings health and life in the lower cauldron of the body generative energy is gathered stored tempered refined and transmuted into spirit energy convention is the enemy of the free body and mind Dylan wrote don't follow leaders watch your parking meters Steve Jonas wrote wear tradition out Pound wrote throw out the iamb Gertrude Stein wrote roast potatoes for Kerouac wrote that god is Pooh Bear Julia writes with her proposed Thanksgiving dinner menu no turkey again this year that is known as convention is the enemy of what we eat she says that her writing is for her readers to think about themselves walk Old Thompson

Road in West Gloucester trail muddy and wet mud sucks feet down over ankles shoes and bottoms of jeans caked never seen so many honey mushrooms they swarm the bottoms of the oak trees prevent any hen-of-the-woods from growing drive to Old Salem Road in Ravenswood where Gerrit Julia and I picked so many hen-of-the-woods over the years at the base of the same oak trees find a hen in perfect form several others too old and waterlogged up the granite hill over the huge boulders thick thorn patches tearing at my legs no hens at the regular spots visit John and Cecilia at the house they invite me for supper Amanda drops over food and conversation then long dark drive from Cape Ann back to the city clean the hen-of-the-woods saute in butter and olive oil freezer pack in separate servings wake to forty-five student essays chip away at them for several hours post assignments for the week run errands do chores cook tomato sauce with ground beef Italian sausages and wild mushrooms over rigatoni she writes too lonely in my long death I have returned to suffer again and how she brought pine needles home from her walk at dusk and made tea and called it Tea of a Lover Jim writes from Rafe's Chasm the bluefish have been running someone picked the hen-of-the-woods that were on the trail I write the Great Clod continues to burden me with form ATM eats my debit card call bank wait thirty-five minutes for a voice another forty minutes before I am told I must go to my branch they're unable to cancel the card drive to bank wait fifteen minutes to speak with a representative who takes care of everything apologizes for the inconvenience of nearly two hours out of my day to fix the problem of their machine eating my card Nick and Shira send photo of Rosie holding up huge hen-of-the-woods they found and spent the evening cleaning and prepping it finish two classes worth of essays on Frederick Douglass now begin another class's essays on *Animal Farm* creative writing student keeps asking me about how she can get published and paid for her work she's only written one short story I suggest she write ten before she send any out but she doesn't want to hear it neighbors have chickens clucking all day long other neighbors board dogs bark all day long too crowded in the city for chickens and dog kennels too many people care only about their wants and needs when autumn arrives summer must go along with butterflies and bees somewhere a lonely poet grieves leaves this world for another and their sorrows behind having seen through this world to enter a sacred order it is written that years ago a woodcutter climbed a tree and fell never to reach the ground as far as anyone could tell this is known as falling and never reaching the ground I wish I could put a full stop to the conversation in my mind no matter how hard I try the tape continues to roll in 1630 Indian trader John Woolrich was the first white man to cross the Neck from Charlestown and settle into what became known as Somerville this very afternoon not one parking spot available on Oxford Street this is known as progress to some lost in the whirl of cosmic dust spit back out left to rot the crux of the story is lost in unrecognizable words that no one understands sounds express emotion the Way in motion endlessly tuned to frequencies heretofore unknown this is known as songs for which there are titles

quale [kwa-lay]: *Eng.* n 1. A property (such as hardness) considered apart from things that have that property. 2. A property that is experienced as distinct from any source it may have in a physical object. *Ital.* pron.a. 1. Which, what. 2. Who. 3. Some. 4. As, just as.

www.ingramcontent.com/pod-product-compliance
Lightning Source LLC
Chambersburg PA
CBHW021012090426
42738CB00007B/758